Dare To Trust

Cut the Shorelines ...
See the Works of the Lord

Edward Powell

Edward Powell
Nahum 1:7

XULON PRESS

Dedication

I am indebted to the Pastors, Missionaries, Teachers, and Godly Layman that have been used of the Holy Spirit to impact my life and leave an indelible impression upon my heart. Their writings, their spoken word, and their Christ-like lives, have penetrated my heart. They have helped me to be established in the faith, created a thirst for His Word, and challenged me to "walk worthy of the Lord unto all." They have eternally enriched my life!

Table of Contents

Acknowledgments

I have endeavored to acknowledge any illustration or excerpt from the original source that was used in any of the devotions. Some material has been retold over the years, and there was no way to trace its origin. If I have failed to give credit to anyone for any work that has been used, I request your forgiveness. Please contact the Author at his email address, powellvilla@cfl.rr.com and corrections will be made prior to additional printing. My sincere appreciation goes to Mary Johnson of Chamblee, Georgia, for her tireless effort and professional expertise in editing these devotions. If this book has been a blessing, encouragement, or challenge to you, I would appreciate hearing from you.

Foreword

*D*ARE TO TRUST is a challenge to every Believer, to put into practice the faith they possess. If our faith is truly planted deep in God's Word and in the sacrificial work of Christ as our Saviour, then what we believe must find manifestation in our walk and life. These devotions explore the reality of our faith, test the commitment of our walk, and whether the Holy Spirit has free and full access in our life. They will bring you to a greater understanding to what Christ said, "If any man will come after me, let him deny himself and take up his cross daily, and follow me." It means you must "cut the shorelines" [those things that hinder and bind you from following Christ without reservation] ... "and see the works of the Lord, and his wonders in the deep." It means DARING TO TRUST HIM in the uncharted waters [those times when you encounter testing, adversity, and trials] when you are challenged to manifest absolute confidence in God. Such crises times reveal whether you are willing to go to the breaking point, and yet not break your steadfast confidence in God's faithfulness and Covenant to you. But it is here that you DARE TO TRUST GOD and see the mighty works of the Lord in your life!

Go Down to the Sea

"They that go down to the sea in ships, that do business in great waters. These see the works of the Lord, and his wonders in the deep." Psalm 107:23, 24

Have you ever ventured into a task, exercised faith and confidence in God, and when it was all over, you humbly said, "Only God could have done that!" It was a thrill to see God do what you could not do. Then you wonder, "Why don't I trust Him that way more often?"

We confine ourselves when we live within the boundaries of our own reasoning, gifts, and abilities and in "the shallow waters" within the safety and security of land. God wants us to focus our expectations on things that are beyond our capabilities, that will stretch our faith and deepen our prayer life, and to live in the daily expectation of seeing "the works of the Lord, and His wonders in the deep." He wants us to launch out into deep, uncharted waters, where faith is our watchword.

God promises an exciting life of faith for those of us who "dare to believe" and are willing to cut the "shore lines" that bind our freedom and confine our liberty. Those who set their sails into the deep waters of the unknown will see His mighty power going before, making the crooked ways straight, parting the sea, and removing the mountains. This is the excitement of a life of faith, daring to launch out into the deep encounters of life with unwavering confidence in the Faithful One. Such ventures reveal our spiritual integrity, test our commitment, and require from us a determined perseverance with complete trust in the Lord. But how glorious the results! Our faith is renewed, our lives become grounded in the Word, and we grow in grace and knowledge of Him. Are you "seeing the works of the Lord" in your life? Are you moved by the "wonders of His mighty power" in the encounters you face?

The curse of the world and the carnal believer is SELF. The aim of Christianity is to "put Christ where man puts Self." His rightful place is on the throne of our hearts as the Lord of our life. "Things" are the "shore lines" that hinder us from discovering the wonders of the deep that can be ours. They hinder us from surrendering unto Him the command of our little ship, letting Him determine the way and chart the course we are to take. Read Luke 5:4-11, where Christ told Peter to "launch out into the deep" that he might catch many fish. When Peter obeyed, many fish were caught. "Henceforth you shall catch men. And when they brought their ships to land, they forsook all and followed him." What happened in the lives of Peter, James, and John through this encounter with the Lord? They saw the Lord in a new dimension.

They knew Him as a great teacher, a master communicator, possibly the "One Sent from God," but now they saw Him as the LORD OF THEIR LIFE! When we give Him our all, He gives us His all. We will then "do business in great waters, and see his wonders in the deep!" What an exciting venture of faith, seeing God work in and through our lives in ways beyond all we can ask or think! What a Challenge! Dare to Believe!

The Prisoners Heard Them

"And at midnight Paul and Silas prayed, and sang praises unto God: and the prisoners heard them. And suddenly there was a great earthquake." Acts 16:25

What a blessed release comes to us when we recognize the Source of our Sufficiency, the Fountainhead from which the refreshing waters of Life flow, when we stop "striving to be" and simply turn our all over to the Lord. This is one of the most difficult things we face as Believers. For some reason, we continue to think, WE MUST MAKE IT HAPPEN, when the Lord stands by "waiting to make it happen." First, He must have the resignation of our weakness and inability committed to His Ability. He must "be" and He must "do" in our lives the things that make us "instruments of praise" to glorify Him. Our efforts are like notes of discord – harsh, loud, disruptive, and completely out of tune. We must lay the whole of our lives into the hands of the Master, for His use and under His Control.

Paganini, the world-renowned violinist, was the featured artist at Carnegie Hall. The Hall was packed with excited and enthusiastic music lovers who appreciated the artistry of this master violinist, acclaimed around the world for his musical genius. He appeared on stage and after the applause, quietly placed his instrument under his chin, only to make the alarming discovery that it was not his treasured Stradivarius. He excused himself and went to his dressing room to retrieve his famous violin, only to find that someone had stolen it and replaced it with a cheap replica. After a moment of shock and reflection, he returned to the stage and told the audience of his misfortune. Then he said, "Ladies and gentlemen, with this cheap secondhand fiddle, I will show you that the music is not in the instrument, but in the soul." He then began to play as never before, and that secondhand violin poured forth music that completely enthralled the audience. They were captivated by the music from the Master. The applause seemed endless with excitement and appreciation!

Servants of Christ are challenged, amidst the trying conditions and discords of life, the discouragements and disappointments, not to let the "music" resounding from our lives be conditioned by external things that we encounter from day to day. The music will be a "melody born in the soul" when we surrender our efforts of striving and struggling to the ONE who can turn them into songs in the night and songs of praise that ONLY HE CAN PRODUCE! The Lord is longing to use you AS YOU ARE, but under the MASTERY OF HIS ARTISTRY!

Was it not the experience of Paul and Silas? Bound in stocks of confinement in a dark and dingy prison, beaten with many stripes, but rejoicing in the Lord, they lifted up their heart in "songs of praise." Was this their doing? No, it was the Spirit of the Lord manifesting His Life through them! His Strength made a reality in their weakness, His Comfort in their concern, His Freedom in their confinement, and His Victory in their defeat. The Lord was in control! The results were glorious. The Lord wants to take the secondhand residue of our lives and make something beautiful, a melody of praise that will glorify Him. But HE MUST DO IT. WE CAN'T. Place "your fiddle" in the MASTER'S HAND. LET HIM PRODUCE ETERNAL MUSIC FROM YOUR LIFE!

Remember All the Way God Has Led You

"Thou shall remember all the way which the Lord your God led you these forty years in the wilderness, to humble thee, and to prove thee, to know what was in thine heart, whether thou wouldest keep his commandments, or no."
Deuteronomy 8:2

God seeks to "draw us unto Himself" in an intimate relationship so that we might share His companionship. He desires to reveal Himself unto us as the All-Sufficient Mighty God. He wanted to awaken the hearts of His chosen people Israel to all they would encounter when they entered Canaan to claim their inheritance. He wanted them to know the "why" of their wilderness journey.

Moses said unto them, "Remember all the way which the Lord thy God has led you these forty years in the wilderness!" How soon we forget the mercy and grace of God. He wanted their "hearts to obey Jehovah." Moses at the end of the Passover Feast and the Feast of Unleavened Bread gave these significant words! As they observed the Passover Feast, they were to remember that it was by sprinkling the blood of the Paschal Lamb on the lintels of the doors that they were delivered from the sword of the destroying angel. It was deliverance by God's grace, mercy, and love. Preceding this was the Feast of Unleavened Bread, which was the cleansing process. No leaven was to be in the house as they observed the Passover Feast. Leaven was symbolic of sin, and God wanted their hearts cleansed from all sin, every impediment removed as they remembered the miraculous deliverance they had from their bondage in Egypt. It was in vain to keep the Passover if they did not keep the Feast of Unleavened Bread.

Three things express the "why" of their wilderness journey. First, to "humble you." God wanted to reveal their pride, ego, self-sufficiency, and independence. Second, to "prove you." God sought to reveal the sincerity of their faith. Was it a faith that had relevance to their daily lives? Third, to "know what was in their hearts." They needed to realize the deceitfulness and degradation of their hearts. "The heart is deceitful above all things, who can know it." God sought to orchestrate their lives to be upright in their love of Him. In response, God said, "The Lord has declared this day that you are His people, His treasured possession as He promised, that you are to keep all His commands. He has declared that He will set you in praise, fame and honour, high above all the nations He has made; you will be a people holy unto the Lord your God as He promised."

What He covenanted with Israel, He has covenanted with us today. The evidence of God's grace and mercy to Israel is great, but it is nothing compared to the manifestation of His love to us in giving His only begotten Son to pay the debt of our sin. There is no way to comprehend the Love of God. How should we respond to so great a love? What should be the hallmark of our life? What should characterize the whole of our being? The same as He wanted from Israel: "obedience to His will in the whole of our life," not counting anything unworthy of our notice or too difficult for us to perform, that we might have "the mind of Christ in all things." The life we live must declare "whose we are and whom we serve."

Adopted Into the Family of God

"For you have not received the spirit of bondage again to fear; but you have received the Spirit of adoption, whereby we cry, Abba, Father." Romans 8:15

Many Christians believe that when they trust Christ as their Lord and Saviour, God's work in their life is complete. Our reconciliation to God and our salvation are complete, but our Spiritual Journey, our walk and warfare, and our life as a follower of Christ have just begun! Paul challenges the Christians to "grow in grace," to "walk worthy of the Lord," to "study to show yourself approved unto God a workman that needs not to be ashamed, rightly dividing the Word of Truth." There is much to be done so that we may be strong, steadfast, and mature in our spiritual life.

Paul says, "You were once darkness." The word "darkness" in the Scriptures implies sin, misery, ignorance, unsaved, the mind of the unbeliever. He is blind to the things of God, which must be "spiritually discerned." He has no concept of God as Holy, Just, and Righteous. He does not know that his heart is totally alienated from God because of his sin. He has no sense of his need for salvation because of the blindness of his heart. Unsaved men not only are in darkness, but are darkness itself.

Then Paul says, "But they are now light in the Lord." What happened? "They turned from darkness unto light, from the power of Satan unto God, the eyes of their understanding being enlightened." They have been adopted into the Family of God by the power of the Holy Spirit, wherefore they cry, "Abba Father." As children of our parents, we are the result of the natural process of reproduction. But one who is adopted is brought into a family wholly by grace. He shares all the privileges and benefits of the family and is made an heir to the father's wealth. Notice, it was not because he desired to be a member of the family, not because he merited adoption, not because he could obtain such a relationship, but because he has been adopted into the family ALL BY GRACE! The father did everything necessary to make him a full member of the family. The father accepted him AS HIS VERY OWN! What a beautiful picture of our adoption into the Family of God, who has given us a seat at His Table. This thought was brought home strikingly to me several years ago when I was one of 25 selected guests for a dinner honoring the retirement of Mr. Charles Haviland, heir and CEO of the Haviland China Co. It was elegant and classy to the utmost. One prominent couple from France, Mr. and Mrs. Rothschild, members of one of the wealthiest families in the world, were close friends of the Havilands. Seats were assigned, and I was seated next to Mrs. Rothschild – next to wealthy French Royalty. She was a beautiful, charming, and gracious lady, friendly and engaging in conversation. I felt very honored, somewhat in awe, to be given such a privileged seat.

Then I thought, ONE DAY I'll be seated at the FATHER'S TABLE, next to the King of kings and Lord of lords, because I have been adopted into the Family of God! I am one of His Very Own! Through adoption, I am an heir of God and a joint heir with Jesus Christ! All by His Grace! The Father did everything necessary to adopt me and to accept me "in the Beloved."

The Word Was Made Flesh

"In the beginning was the Word, and the Word was with God, and the Word was God. And the Word was made flesh, and dwelt among us." John 1:1, 14

How can we possibly conceive of or understand the tremendous Truth in these verses? We can only exclaim from our hearts, "How inconceivably great is the condescension of our mighty God!" To think that God should take upon Him the form of a servant and become man, and should make Himself the Surety and Substitute for His own rebellious creatures, is beyond our uttermost thought. But He is God, and therefore He can do it. He is God; therefore I believe all that He has done.

What is the significance of John's declaration of THE WORD? Comparing it to the name given to the Scriptures, "The Word of God," we may discover the force and impact of its meaning and importance. The Scriptures reveal God's mind, express His will, and unveil His plan, purpose and revelation for man. They make known His attributes and His perfections. They lay bare the Heart of God, His condescending love, His matchless grace, His infinite mercy, and our blessed hope!

"And the WORD was God." He was not an "idea" of God or a "divine spark" placed within mankind. He was not an expression of God, but God Himself manifested to man. He not only revealed God, but was God Himself revealed. As the WORD, He did not come into being, or begin to be, but HE (Jesus Christ) was with God from all eternity, before time began. Therefore, He was "without beginning," which means He was eternal. Christ is the One who made the "incomprehensible God, intelligible to mankind." He is the One who declared the Father unto mankind and has purchased our redemption, "was made sin for us, that we might be made the righteousness of God in Him." Though He Himself was eternal, yet He was born "in time." Though He was eternally with God, in infinite condescending Love, He came down and tabernacled with man. Though He was the true and living God, He "made himself of no reputation, and took upon him the form of a servant, and was made in the likeness of man, and became obedient unto death, even the death of the cross."

I believe the complete Word of God, because He revealed it. Nothing less than His finished work on Calvary would be adequate to meet our need and reconcile us to God. He declared, "I am the WAY, the TRUTH, and the LIFE; no man cometh unto the Father, but by me." What unbounded consolation He has provided for sinful man.

I have guilt that nothing but the blood of Christ can wash away. I have corruption that none but the Holy Spirit can subdue and mortify. I have wants that none but an All-Sufficient Saviour can supply. Having Christ as My Saviour, My Friend, My Surety, My Righteousness, My Companion, MY ALL, I have nothing to fear. I Hope in Him, I Believe in Him, I Glory in Him. I make Him my salvation and all my desire. Trusting in Him, I will defy all my enemies. I will anticipate all He has prepared for me in Heaven. "For in Him, and through Him, and to Him, are all things; to whom be glory forever, Amen." "And the WORD was made flesh, and dwelt among us, and we beheld his glory, the glory as of the only begotten of the Father, full of grace and truth." HALLELUJAH!

Our Bodies a Living Sacrifice

"I beseech you therefore, brethren, by the mercies of God, that ye present your bodies a living sacrifice, holy, acceptable unto God, which is your reasonable service." Romans 12:1

The measure, in which Christ has liberty to live in our lives, has a direct relationship to how we will experience His peace, joy, blessing, and power in our lives. Paul says, Because of the tender mercies of God in redeeming you, the most reasonable thing you can do is present your bodies as a "living sacrificial offering", displaying unto others a "holy life acceptable to God." This can only happen when we recognize our nothingness in the light of His All Sufficiency. He becomes the complement of our need, our Source of strength for every task, and the Authority of our life. When we surrender our will to His Sovereignty a radical change begins, and a transforming process proceeds under the control of the Holy Spirit.

When we have tasted the goodness of God, our guilt is replaced by abundant grace; sin's vigorous pull is mortified by the Spirit's power; the circle of self gives way to the Presence of God; pride is turned into love; and a blessed exchange takes place as the "self-life" is replaced by the "Christ-life." We are transformed by HIS POWER and made new creations in Christ to be "conformed into the image of His Son."

This is not a one-time experience that we immediately enter into a life free from the influences of our old nature. When we grow in grace, our Spiritual Journey will be one of becoming like Him. The difficulties in our lives are His way of trying to chisel the old habits and attitudes that are detrimental to a life pleasing to Him. Our old nature seeks to influence us to "our interests, our will, and our way." It is imperative that we daily submit to His Authority and Control, live under His Lordship, and make Him the Sovereign of our life.

We will begin to walk in a new relationship where we experience His presence and power as never before. We will enter into a blessed companionship, an exciting adventure, as we "dare to believe" and exercise childlike faith in the faithfulness of our Mighty God. Prayer will be a precious encounter into the "secret place of His tabernacle." We will see Him going before, preparing the way, and manifesting His power in ways beyond our capacity. Our spiritual journey becomes a life lived in the "reality of His Presence!" Are you a candidate for such a life? Paul says that to present your body as a "living sacrifice, holy, acceptable unto God" is the most reasonable thing you can do. I challenge you to take this step of faith and commitment and let Him do "exceeding abundantly above all you can ask or even think, through the power that works in you." YOU WILL NEVER BE THE SAME!

There are no circumstances beyond God's power. There is nothing so trivial that is beyond His fathomless love! God is interested in every aspect of our life. He came not only to give us life, but that we might have it to the fullest! To hold onto our selfish life is to miss out on all God wants to do in our life. Someone wisely said, "Unless He is the Lord of all, He is not Lord at all." Give Him your all today!

Purge Me... Wash Me... Make Me

"Cleanse me with hyssop, and I will be clean: wash me, and I shall be whiter than snow. Let me hear joy and gladness; let the bones you have crushed rejoice." Psalm 51:7, 8

Not until we see ourselves in our pitiful, corrupt "self" before the holiness and righteousness of God, do we cry out as David. He says, "For troubles without number surround me; my sins have overtaken me, and I cannot see. They are more than the hairs of my head, and my heart fails within me." Possibly he was thinking how sin had consumed him when he planned to have Uriah killed in battle so he could have Bathsheba for himself. Certainly, he would not think those actions were foreign to his deceived heart; rather, it was an indication of the "extreme depravity of his own heart." What inward grief and conviction must have reigned when Nathan said to David, "You are the man," establishing his sin, not only before man, but also before God. David is deeply convicted and completely crushed with guilt and shame.

He acknowledges his sin before God and seeks to be restored to the Holy Communion and companionship he had previously with Jehovah. He cries out to God, "Purge me with hyssop and I shall be [ceremonially] clean." Hyssop was the little shrub with which the blood and water of purification were applied. This he needed, as he bares himself before God, declaring all his hopes and fears, his grief and consolations. Then he says, "Wash me [continually] and I shall [in reality] be whiter than snow." A once-and-for-all cleansing was not enough; he needed daily cleansing. Then he prevails upon the grace of God, "Let me hear joy and gladness; let the bones you have crushed rejoice." To David, who had known such privileged, intimate communion with God, just to be purged and washed was not enough. He wanted to be restored completely; he wanted his repenting soul to once again sing aloud the clear "songs of deliverance!" The cry of his heart was, "Restore unto me the joy of your salvation and grant me a willing spirit, to sustain me." He was aware of the penetrating, heart-searching eye of God, which revealed that he had been "weighed in the balance, and had been found wanting!" It is the same with us: With broken heart and contrite spirit, we can find deliverance!

It was with tender compassion, with anxious care, and with joyful satisfaction that God dealt with David. Well might we wonder how it must have been to have God's Divine wisdom seeking to lead him, His Almighty Power ready to uphold him, His Fathomless Mercy interceding for his sins and frailties, and His Faithfulness making a reality His promises in David's behalf! Is it any wonder that when David considered these things, he was compelled to cry out, "Why art thou cast down, O my soul, and why art thou disquieted within me? HOPE THOU IN GOD, for I shall yet praise him, who is the health of my countenance, and my God." (Psalm 42:11) The more we are sensitive to our guilt and helplessness, the more God is ready to help, restore, forgive, and deliver us and "make the bones he has crushed rejoice." A contrite heart he will not despise. His arms of mercy and grace are ready to reconcile and restore! "Because of the Lord's great love, we are not consumed, for his compassions never fail. They are new every morning. Great is your faithfulness!" Dare to believe. God is on the Throne!

Possessed by Christ

"I am crucified with Christ: nevertheless I live; yet not I, but Christ liveth in me: and the life I now live in the flesh I live by the faith of the Son of God, who loved me, and gave himself for me." Galatians 2:20

*W*hen we receive Christ as Lord and Saviour, we have access to all He has provided for us. We possess His life and nature, we are made a new creation in Christ, and we are positional in Christ. But there is more! A radical change takes place when Christ possesses us, when Christ has access to all of us! Paul said, "It is not I that lives, but CHRIST LIVES IN ME!" He has possession of all there is of me, the whole of my being. He is in Sovereign Control of my life.

When Christ possesses us, the self-imposed walls we have built around us suddenly disappear. Gone! Those thoughts that generated "our image and fostered our future" take on an entirely new perspective when "Christ possesses us." Consider how Paul looked at his tribulations after he became a Believer. Paul could have said, "I have served God for years. I have travelled, been beaten, suffered at the hands of evil men, been shipwrecked, stoned, left for dead, falsely accused, robbed, in pain, weary, cold, hungry, thirsty, in nakedness, and in peril on every side! Why has all this come to me? It's not fair!" But there was not a word of self-pity or any complaint for the things he endured. WHY? Because Paul not only possessed the in-living Christ, but CHRIST POSSESSED ALL OF PAUL!

Paul says, I want you to see that all these things that I have encountered since I became a Believer have happened "unto the furtherance of the Gospel." He saw God's Hand in it all. Wow! Wouldn't it be wonderful if we had such a focus of Christ in our life? I have news for you: WE CAN! We serve the same Lord, who is the same yesterday, today, and forever! It's a matter of CHRIST POSSESSING THE WHOLE OF OUR LIFE! Paul does not focus on the trials and sufferings of his life; they were but steppingstones that God permitted so that he might be "conformed unto the image of His Son." Paul says, "In all these things we are more than conquerors through him that loved us." To be "more than a conqueror" is not only to be victorious over the enemy, but to take the "very elements of battle" that were used against us and make them advantageous for our own use. Let me illustrate.

The printer and evangelist Dr. William Moon of Brighton, England, was stricken with blindness at the height of is career. He said, "Lord, I accept this blindness from you. Help me to use it for your glory, that at your coming, you may receive your own with great joy." Then God enabled him to invent the Moon Alphabet for the Blind, by which untold thousands have been able to read the Scriptures and many of them have been gloriously saved.

God did not take away Paul's thorn in the flesh; He did better. Paul mastered that thorn, made it his servant, and received the power to be "more than a conqueror." The Ministry of Thorns often has been far greater than the Ministry of Thrones.

Oh that we might move to higher ground... to a new and living way... to the exciting venture of being filled with the fullness of God. From having "access to Christ" to BEING POSSESSED BY CHRIST! What a difference!

With God Nothing Is Impossible

"Then said Mary unto the angel, how shall this be, seeing I know not a man? ... For with God nothing shall be impossible." Luke 1:34, 37

*D*o you really believe God can or, even more, will do the impossible in your life? The depth of your devotion and commitment to God, the reality of your personal relationship with the Lord, the application of the simple yet profound truths in His Word, will be in direct proportion to whether we believe what God says and act upon it. Many simply give an intellectual assent to what God has revealed in His Word and discount the "supernatural nature of God."

When Mary was approached by the angel and told that she would bear the Son of God, what was her reaction? Yes, she was startled, and probably dumbfounded, that such a thing was even possible. But when the angel told her how it would happen, there was an immediate, unhesitating, full and complete faith that God was going to do the "impossible." Why, do we find it so difficult to trust God to do things that are beyond ourselves? I think it's because we limit our thinking and vision to the self-imposed walls of our understanding. We are finite; God is infinite. Our abilities and gifts are confined to our limitations; God's ability and power are fathomless. But everything changes when we allow God to enter the picture and give Him the Authority and Control of our lives.

Many times throughout the Scriptures we find two transforming words: BUT GOD! When we come across these two words, everything changes. All that is written after these two words supersedes everything that was said before. Read Ephesians 2:1-3, which describes our lost and ruined condition walking without God – "the children of wrath." Then we read "BUT GOD," and it reveals the mighty transformation that takes place when He becomes our Lord and Saviour. But there is more!

When we believe, He wants to take His rightful place on the "throne of our life." When, with surrendered heart and will, we turn our lives over to His Lordship and walk in childlike trust in His all-sufficiency, we begin to see the "wonders of His power!" Let me give you an example from my own life. I interrupted my senior year of high school and attended Wheaton College in 1943. God broke through, and a "mighty revival" took place on campus that has had worldwide results ever since. I made "my surrender" to His Lordship, and my life was changed forever! He was preparing me for a tragedy 21 months ahead, to experience His presence and power in an awesome way. I was in the Army as a machine gunner with the 1st Division, fighting in the Hurtgen Forest in Germany. A terrifying artillery barrage by the Germans left me critically wounded. Both of my arms and one leg were almost blown off, BUT GOD gave me a "song in the night" as I lay on a stretcher across the hood of a jeep at midnight as it made its way to the first aid tent. I thought, "This is it; I'm going to die." I started singing, "Only trust Him, only trust Him, He will save you, He will save you now." God gave me perfect peace. Our limitations are occasions for us to experience His fathomless sufficiency to meet us at the point of our need. "For with God, NOTHING SHALL BE IMPOSSIBLE." Our responsibility is obedience; the results are His! DARE TO BELIEVE!

Other Fell Into Good Ground

"But other fell into good ground, and brought forth fruit, some an hundredfold, some sixtyfold, some thirtyfold." Matthew 13:8

*J*esus often spoke unto the people in a parable to illustrate, through familiar, everyday experiences in life, spiritual truth for application to their lives. Being largely an agricultural society, He is here using an account of a sower casting seed over a field. Scattering the seed by hand, he was throwing it in all directions. He realized that some of the seed would fall on unproductive ground, but he expected most to fall on fertile ground and bring a harvest. Jesus gives four examples that relate to the reception of the Gospel as it is spread among the people.

"When he sowed, some seed fell by the wayside, and the fowls came and ate them up." This relates to those who come under the sound of the Gospel, are attentive, and follow the form and traditions exercised in the service. Their minds are occupied with "other things," plans, business, pleasure, and relationships. They hear but they do not respond nor give place to the Word that is preached. Satan, like the fowls of the air, hovers over them to catch the seed, diverting their minds from the truth.

"Some fell upon stony places, where they had not much earth, and forthwith they sprung up, because they had no deepness of earth."

These hear the Word gladly, but their affections are like a thin layer of earth upon a rock. They are attracted by the "novelty" of the Gospel: It delights their mind, they are moved by the sufferings of Christ, and they are impressed with the promises of God. Immediately, they begin to make a "profession" of faith. However, when tribulation comes, their profession withers and is burnt up, because the seed was never rooted in their understanding or will. "And some fell among thorns: and the thorns sprung up, and choked them." They maintain a regard for the Gospel, associate with believers, and try to be consistent in their character and profession, but the fruit they produce is not "perfect." Their hearts were never purged from the "thorn." Care and pleasures corrode their lives; there is always something they desire more than "real holiness;" there is lack of focus upon God. Therefore, "things" choke out the seed and it is unfruitful.

"But other fell on good ground, and brought forth fruit." These receive the Word with humility, desiring to be instructed, applying the Word to their lives, and having a hunger and thirst in their hearts to grow in grace. They are receptive and responsive to the Holy Spirit and bear "abundant fruit." Let me challenge you. Look within your life. Examine and judge yourself to see which of the four examples characterizes your life the most. Oh that we might "plough into our hearts" the seed of God's Word by faith, meditation, and prayer, and so labor, that there may be a bountiful harvest! May we have the desire to have the seed fall upon good ground and have a receptive heart and responsive spirit. Satan seeks to divert our attention, encumber our lives, and cause us to be unresponsive to every "planting of the seed" in our hearts. May we be sensitive to God seeking to draw us unto Himself that we may be fruitful. It is only as He lives His Life through us that there will be any fruit for eternity and for His glory. "By their fruit shall ye know them."

Neglect Not the Gift

"Neglect not the gift that is in thee... Give thyself wholly to them." 1 Timothy 4:14,15

*G*od has given unto every Believer a gift or gifts that they are responsible for using to His glory through the ministry of the Holy Spirit. The purposes of these gifts are many. Paul mentions three in particular: for the perfecting of the saints, for the work of the ministry, and for the edifying of the body of Christ. Paul challenges every Believer, "Be steadfast, unmoveable, abounding always in the work of the Lord, for as much as ye know that your labor is not in vain in the Lord."

It is important to understand the Source of our gifts. All gifts proceed from and are empowered by the One and Self-Same Spirit, the third person of the Trinity, the Holy Spirit. From the very beginning, and throughout our spiritual journey, it is He who works all in all! We are not to be proud nor boastful of whatever gift we possess. It has been given to us by the Holy Spirit, and will only be effective and fruitful when He is the One who empowers our gift to be used for God's glory.

I often have stood admiring a magnificent building ascending high into the skyline, and have wondered at the countless features that are designed to make it functional and safe. You wonder why this tall structure doesn't fall over when the storms beat against it. Then I am reminded that it was built "one step at a time." Before the superstructure was erected, a very deep hole was dug, prepared, and secured, that formed the foundation upon which everything was to rest. A foreman told me of all the planning, preparation, and content that went into the foundation. I was amazed! Tremendous iron girders, a massive amount of cement, reinforcement of all kinds, all specifically placed, to make certain the foundation would be "absolutely safe" and would secure the building.

Then I thought of the SURE FOUNDATION we have in Christ, and the gifts that He has given unto us. How are these gifts manifested? Do they proceed from a shallow experience we may have had? Do they emerge from a life not enriched with grace, creating pride in some and envy in others? Does our gift contain the insidious seed of selfish interests that results in self-satisfaction?

Oh to have our gift "anchored in" and "secured by" the ROCK OF AGES, deeply planted within the hallowed Grace of God, and undergirded with the Love of God. Then, wherever God places us, in whatever circumstances we find ourselves, the gift from Him will be manifested in meekness and modesty, in forbearance and forgiveness, coming from a heart committed to God. It will be manifested by His Love that will supersede all of our actions, through the power of the Holy Spirit. Oh that we might recognize the gift God has given us, not neglecting it through complacency or unconcern. We have a responsibility before God and will be held accountable to use our gift in the surroundings where God has placed us and unto others that God brings into our path. Is your gift being used for His glory?

The fruitfulness of our life and the effectiveness of the "gift or gifts'" that God has given us will not be measured by the "grandeur of the superstructure" but by the "depth of our lives" that are embedded in the Sure Foundation of Christ.

Abundant Life in Christ

"I am come that they might have life, and that they might have it more abundantly." John 10:10

*W*ho would not like to have an abundant life? Many immediately think of temporal and material blessings that surround us. These are nice and certainly add to the comfort and ease of our lives. But Christ is speaking of an ABUNDANT LIFE that goes much deeper than the things the world strives for and acclaims as important and necessary.

God wants us to know Him, not only as the One who has forgiven us of our sins and is our Saviour, but also to crown Him the LORD OF OUR LIFE! He wants us to declare Him as the Authority and Sovereign of our life by yielding our will in obedience and compliance to His will. It is then our lives will be open and receptive to all He wants to be unto us. We will know in reality the blessings of the Covenant Relationship given to all who live under His Lordship. Let's look at a few blessings that highlight the "Abundant Life in Christ" that He has for His own.

When we accepted Christ as our Saviour, He set His Seal upon us as His peculiar treasure. He sets apart those who are godly for Him. He gives His angels charge over us. God declares that from that day, we are His purchased possessions. God makes known to us and to the world around us that we are His. He gives unto us the spirit of adoption whereby we cry "Abba Father." The Holy Spirit assures us that we are children of God. He enables us to walk as Christ walked. He empowers us to shine as a light in the midst of a crooked and a perverse world. He makes us a new creation in Christ by His transforming power. He gives unto us the blessed hope of eternal life. He will make us high above all people in praise, in name, and in honor. He has bestowed His love upon us and we are called the sons of God. He has prepared crowns and kingdoms that we may sit with Him in Eternity and be partakers of His Glory forever!

This, and infinitely more than words can express, God has prepared for those that love Him and embrace His Covenant of Life and Peace. He pledges His Truth and Faithfulness for the performance of His Word. We need to hearken to His voice, even as the angels did. David wrote, "Bless the Lord, ye his angels that excel in strength, that do His commandments, hearkening unto the voice of His word." We should search His Word and meditate upon it so we may know what He says unto us. Oh that we might have an ear to hear the "still small voice" of the Holy Spirit as He reveals, teaches, and directs our lives in His Way, and to respond without hesitation or reservation. The Covenant that God has made unto us is inconceivable, irrevocable, and beyond our human comprehension. The Eternal Creator of all things, by whom all things consist, and through whom they are held together in His Condescending Love, has reconciled us to Himself and gives us not only Life, but also Life More Abundant! Let me ask you, have you entered in to this blessed relationship with Christ? Are you appropriating what He has purchased for you, this Abundant Life in Christ? Neglect not what is yours by faith. I challenge you: POSSESS YOUR INHERITANCE!

In All Your Ways Acknowledge Him

"Trust in the Lord with all your heart, and lean not on your own understanding. In all your ways acknowledge him, and he will make your paths straight." Proverbs 3:5, 6

Many Believers are living under a "spiritual illusion" rather than in the "reality of a personal relationship" with the Lord. They conclude that their whole relationship with God, with Jesus Christ as their Saviour, and with the indwelling presence of the Holy Spirit, is wrapped up in an "act once performed" when they were saved, rather than in a "life to be lived" after their salvation in the power of the Holy Spirit. Their attitude is that having found Him as Saviour, they no longer need to seek Him. Being "born again" is the BEGINNING of our Spiritual Journey. We need to grow in grace and in the knowledge of His Word, becoming mature in our spiritual life.

David's Psalms ring out with the cry of the seeker and resound with the glad song of the finder. Our beloved "hymns of the faith" were born in the fires of trial and adversity by those who found strength, comfort, and hope in an All-Sufficient Saviour. They went through those devastating encounters daring to trust Him. The "reality of our faith" is born when we cast all our care upon Him. It is then we see His Mighty Hand intercede for us in ways that are completely beyond us. It is a life of trust and obedience in a Living Saviour, the Sovereign of our life.

If we are to mature spiritually and come to a deeper experience in "knowing' God," altering our circumstances is not God's first priority. His first concern is to ALTER OUR HEARTS and then He will enable us to deal with the needs on the outside. He wants us to learn to lean on Him and to trust Him in our trials, not to seek deliverance from the trials. It is in the trials that we learn to trust, abandon ourselves unto Him, and come to know Him as never before. Can there be a more blessed experience than to be confronted with devastating circumstances, to pray and trust Him, and to see Him do what no other one can do? We will cry out with David, "Bless the Lord O my soul and all that is within me; Bless His Holy Name." We begin to know and live in the reality of our faith, applying what we believe to every phase of our life. Our Spiritual Journey is one of "becoming" in the image of His Son. It is the process of His plan for each of us.

He gave His Life *for* us, that He might give His Life *to* us, so that He might live His Life *through* us. Paul said, "I consider everything but loss compared to the surpassing greatness of knowing Christ Jesus my Lord, for whose sake I have lost all things. I consider them as rubbish that I may gain Christ and be found in him, not having a righteousness of my own that comes from the law, but that which comes from God and is by faith. I want to know Christ and the power of his resurrection and the fellowship of his sufferings, becoming like him in his death, to attain to the resurrection from the dead." From commitment to Christ, we follow with perseverance and pursue with purpose, "Forgetting what is behind and straining toward what is ahead, I press toward the goal to win the prize for which Christ has called me heavenward in Christ."

Let Us Make Man

"And God said, Let us make man in our image, after our likeness." Genesis 1:26

*S*ince man was created unique and perfect, in the image of God, after His likeness; able to discern good and evil and able to exercise his own will accordingly; created as a free moral agent; put in an environment that abundantly meets his every need; blessed beyond measure in walking with God in the cool of the day... WHAT HAPPENED? Given all of these abundant, positive blessings, how could anything go wrong?

Satan used the same approach with Eve that he uses in the lives of so many today. He planted the insidious "seed of doubt." Eve was beguiled by the subtleness of Satan. Did he try to persuade her to turn her back on God? No, he simply said, "Hath God said?" He caused her to doubt the verity of God's Word. Surely, God has made some mistake by directing you not to eat of "this tree." Surely, with all that God has provided, He would not inflict such a heavy judgment on you for so slight an offense. How could God forbid you to eat from this one tree, when countless other trees are here? "Surely, you shall not die." Oh how clever and beguiling Satan was. How cunningly he diverted her attention from God and all of His provisions to thinking that God was withholding something good from her.

What was Satan trying to do? He was instilling doubt in her heart that "God would not do what He said He would do." People say today, "A good God would not send people to Hell. After all, look at all the good things people do. He certainly wouldn't inflict so great a judgment on man for the few things he might do that are just little sins." You see how this same argument, this same insidious approach by Satan, invades mankind today? What is our problem?

Man seeks to bring God down to his own level, to cast God in his own mold of finite, corrupt thinking. He lifts his proud heart and says, "Really, God doesn't mean what He says literally." Man makes a mockery of sin, lives as if God doesn't exist, and doesn't hesitate to exercise his will in fulfilling the desires of his lust. WHY? Because he has no concept of the Majesty of God, His Holiness, His Righteousness, and His Justice. He casts aside the immutability of His Word. He does not accept or believe that God has a Standard of Truth and Justice that will not be violated. He chooses to violate and voluntarily transgress the very Love, Grace, and Mercy by which God seeks to redeem him from his sin. He is consumed with only one consideration, "personal gratification," without any thought of God who created him.

David, meditating on the infinite greatness of God, exclaims, "What is man that you art mindful of him, the son of man that you care for him?" Who are we, that in any wise should even enter the thoughts of God? But man is persuaded by his own foolish ego and pride, and does not even take God into the equation of his life. How absolutely foolish! Unfortunately, what man thinks will not alter God's plan or purpose. He will only suffer the consequences of "his own choice," meaning eternal separation from a Loving, Merciful, and Gracious God and eternal condemnation in Hell.

Perfecting Holiness

"Having therefore these promises, dearly beloved, let us cleanse ourselves from all filthiness of the flesh and spirit, perfecting holiness in the fear of God." 2 Corinthians 7:1

*M*any Believers do not have a dedicated commitment to the Lord, which finds expression in a walk and life that is lived circumspectly before others. Many have never been taught from the Word that God has given His decree, "Sanctify yourselves therefore and be ye holy, for I am the Lord your God." Others have been challenged to live such a life, but have shunned it, unwilling to surrender and make a commitment to the Lord. Paul had this problem in Corinth. He saw in the walk and worship of many new converts, the sentiments and habits from an old lifestyle. He says, "What? Know ye not that your body is the temple of the Holy Ghost which is in you, which ye have of God, and ye are not your own? For ye are bought with a price; therefore glorify God in your body, and in your spirit, which are God's."

Average Christians have no concept of the reality of being indwelt by the Holy Spirit. Their spiritual life depends largely upon their efforts to maintain their walk and worship. They live on the perimeter of all God wants to do in and through them. Christ died for us, that He might manifest His Life through us.

Paul is pleading with these Believers, "that they receive not the grace of God in vain." He cries out, "O ye Corinthians, our mouth is open to you, our heart is enlarged, be ye also enlarged." In other words, enter into all God has for you and all He wants to do in you. You are the temple in which dwells the Spirit of God. So yield yourselves to Christ so that He can live His life through you. Not only separate yourselves from all that's unclean, but also sanctify yourselves unto Him. And what will He do? "For ye are the temple of the living God; as God hath said, I will dwell in them, and walk in them, and I will be their God, and they shall be my people. I will receive you, and will be a Father unto you, and ye shall be my sons and daughters, says the Lord." This is the exalted position of every Believer. Who can comprehend this? God not only has redeemed us, but he "indwells" us with His Spirit! This is Infinite Condescending Love!

Paul challenges them, as he does us. "Having therefore these promises, let us cleanse ourselves, perfecting holiness in the fear of God." The promises in His Word become effective only when they dwell in our hearts. As we appropriate them with a committed faith, they become "real and operational" in our walk and worship. How can we perfect "holiness in the fear of God?" In awe and profound reverence, "Work out your own salvation in fear and trembling." Delight yourselves in His Presence. Depend upon His care and provision. Have a zeal for His glory. Be sensitive to the working of the Holy Spirit as He probes, cleanses, leads, and reveals God's Word to us.

May God give us a hunger and thirst for an intimate relationship with Christ and the commitment to be diligent in studying His Word and applying it to our lives. Desiring above all things that the whole of our being be filled with the fullness of His Presence, so He will perfect holiness in us! May He be magnified in you!

God's Refreshing Spring

"He that hath mercy on them shall lead them, even by the springs of water shall, he guide them." Isaiah 49:10

*O*ne of the great blessings in life is coming to the Fountain of Living Waters and being Refreshed, Renewed, and Restored by the Presence and Power of God. I'm sure you can testify to the times in your life when you were weary, burdened down with care, and physically and emotionally weak; when seemingly there was no way out but up, and you found those refreshing waters of God that brought peace of heart and soul.

David knew about those waters when, as a shepherd, he often led his sheep over the hills of Palestine. Later, he found those waters a solace of rest and peace, reviving his life from the continual pursuit of his enemies. David said, "He leads me beside the still waters, he restores my soul." As he came to those waters, God said unto him, "Be still and know that I am God."

In this quiet time, God brings to our heart a realization of our utter inability to handle our problems in our own strength. In the desert stretches of our spiritual journey, God has His refreshing springs. We see an impregnable rock and cannot imagine that it marks a delightful oasis. We see a flinty place and cannot conceive that it hides a refreshing fountain. It is in the quietness of His presence that He wants us to know, "My thoughts are not your thoughts, neither are your ways my ways, says the Lord. For as the heavens are higher than the earth, so are my ways higher than your ways and my thoughts than yours."

We will also find resignation of our will to His. He says to us, "Cast all of your care [anxiety, heartache, problems] on me, for I care for you." You cannot handle this need, but I can. Put your trust in me. Let me shoulder the burden; let me be your sufficiency and give deliverance. When we resign our hearts to His control and our will to His Sovereignty, there comes a blessed release from our need. He gives us the assurance that "He is able to do exceeding abundantly above all we can ask or even think." His peace that passes human understanding becomes a reality to us.

Then the challenge comes for us to exercise faith in the Might of His Power. God has given us many wonderful promises of what He wants to do in and through us, and has revealed what He is able to do for us in our many devastating circumstances. But until we appropriate what He has provided, His promises are useless to us. They have been given us to lay hold of by faith, to take possession of, to make our own, that He may make true unto us the resources of His Power. God said, "Call upon me and I will answer you, and I will show you great and mighty things which you know not." Wow! Let me ask you: Have you been to the Fountain of Living Waters and been refreshed, renewed, and restored? Come to the fountain that never runs dry.

Jesus said, "He that believeth on me, as the scripture hath said, out of his innermost being shall flow rivers of living water." Oh that we might say with David, "I will lift up my eyes unto the hills from where my help comes. My help comes from the Lord."

David Faithful to His Covenant with Jonathan

"And David said, Is there yet any that is left of the house of Saul, that I may show him kindness for Jonathan's sake?" 2 Samuel 9:1

*S*aul and his two sons had been slain in battle and David is now King. Instead of using his royal power maliciously, he extends kindness. The beautiful covenant between David and Jonathan finds a reason to exercise lovingkindness from the heart of David. He seeks to extend pity to the descendant of his archenemy, to befriend one who might well have feared death at the hands of David. He takes the initiative to find any descendant of Saul that he may show kindness for Jonathan's sake.

The one who now receives kindness at the hands of the King is so blessed, not because of anything he has done, or any worthiness he possesses, but wholly because of a Covenant Promise by David to Jonathan. "And Ziba said unto the King, Jonathan has yet a son, which is lame on his feet. Now when Mephibosheth, the son of Jonathan, the son of Saul, was come to David, he fell on his face and did reverence." David's words were full of grace as he addressed Mephibosheth, "Fear not, for I will surely show you kindness for Jonathan your father's sake, and will restore to you all the land of Saul your father, and you shall eat at my table continually." What a moving scene! Mephibosheth "bowed himself and said, what is your servant that you should look upon such a dead dog that I am?"

The mercy and grace shown by David moved to contrition the heart of this crippled, outcast son of Jonathan. It brought a deep consciousness that he was utterly unworthy yet the recipient of matchless grace. There was life for him, for David refused to take revenge upon him for the injustice and cruelty he suffered from Saul. He returned good for evil, love for hate, grace instead of justice, and mercy instead of wrath. David's words "fear not" put to rest all anxiety, quieted his heart, and set him at perfect ease in the presence of the King. There was an inheritance. "All that pertained to Saul and to all his house" was restored unto him, after it had been lost to his family. Then David extends to him a most gracious gift: "You shall eat bread at my table continually." What a contrast from being a crippled outcast in Lodebar [place of no pasture] to being seated at the King's Table, not once, but continually! The capstone of David's grace are his words: "As for Mephibosheth, said the king, He shall eat at my table AS ONE OF THE KING'S SONS!" Not as an alien, or a stranger, or a servant, or a guest, but as a Member of the Royal Family. AS ONE OF THE KING'S SONS!

What a magnificent picture of our redemption! We, who deserve nothing but the judgment of God, are taken in by His Love and Grace, given an eternal inheritance, and made to sit at the Father's Table forever! Cleansed by the blood of Christ; reconciled unto God and given a peace that passes understanding, joy that is unspeakable and full of glory, and mercy that endures forever; accepted in the Beloved; made an Heir of God and a Joint Heir with Christ; indwelt by the Holy Spirit ... ALL BY THE MATCHLESS GRACE OF OUR LOVING LORD! His Grace is greater than all our sin. Marvelous, Matchless, Infinite Grace!

He Went on His Way Rejoicing

"And when they were come up out of the water, the Spirit of the Lord caught away Philip, that the eunuch saw him no more: and he went on his way rejoicing." Acts 8:39

The effectiveness of a faithful witness, empowered by the Holy Spirit, is like the ripples on a pond when you throw a rock in the middle: They multiply over and over again in all directions. Four major results of Stephen's martyrdom are still effective today!

First, on the very day of his martyrdom, widespread persecution of Christians was initiated. Believers in Jerusalem fled in fear in every direction. It was by no accident of fate that a zealous young Pharisee by the name of Saul witnessed the martyrdom of Stephen. Saul was a learned man and could understand the reasoning of Stephen as he addressed the ruling elders. He saw the steadfast way Stephen faced his accusers, the courageous way he died, his complete resignation to God. He saw grace "manifested beyond measure" as Stephen prayed for his enemies. God indelibly inscribed these things upon the heart of Saul, who soon was converted and began a ministry anointed of God that has influenced the world ever since!

Second, Saul was determined to stamp out this insidious Christian movement, dragging Christians from their homes, torturing them, and putting them in prison. But God caused the Believers to be scattered into the surrounding countries with their faithful witness, and the Gospel was spread in an unprecedented way. In trying to extinguish the flames of Christianity, opponents scattered the sparks far and wide, increasing the scope of its fire and the intensity of its message. It has spread around the world ever since by the mighty power of God.

Third, the Holy Spirit came upon Philip, and led him to preach the Gospel in Samaria, a place and a people who despised the Jews. Likewise, the Jews regarded the Samaritans as unclean, unbelieving, and despicable. Intense hostility was constantly evident between the two. This was the first recorded instance of the Gospel being "taken to and received by" the Samaritans. A tremendous spiritual awakening broke out in Samaria, and many believed and were received into the faith. The Gospel was implanted in their lives, and churches were founded.

Fourth, Philip is divinely led to travel a desert road from Jerusalem to Gaza, where he encounters an Ethiopian Eunuch, the treasurer for the Ethiopian ruler Candace. The Jewish law forbade a Eunuch from entering the Temple. God planned to reach this influential man by sending Philip personally to interpret the Scriptures and reveal unto him the way of eternal life. The Eunuch was saved, baptized, and used mightily by God in spreading the Gospel. Significant? Tremendously so! The Gospel had never been proclaimed in Ethiopia, which at that time was the most barbarian country in the world. As the Eunuch returned to his country, many churches were raised up "through his life." The Gospel was spread to all of Western Europe, to every country in the known world!

These four significant things changed the course of the whole world! It all started through the courageous, faithful witness of one who was "constrained by the love of God." Man will not stay the Hand of God. Through His Own, He will manifest His power and carry out His plan and purpose. HE IS SOVEREIGN!

Let Us Come Boldly

"Let us therefore come boldly to the throne of grace, that we may obtain mercy and find grace to help in time of need."
Hebrews 4:16

We often wonder why God permits the trials and adversities of life. We become frustrated, impatient, and weary sometimes when we encounter these experiences. But in yielding to His control when they befall us, they become determining factors to develop in us a depth and measure of His grace, love, and mercy we have not known before. For it is in the trial, in the adversity, in our difficulty, and in the darkness of these hours, that the light of His Presence and Power shines brightest.

Prayer becomes a most blessed encounter with God. It is a blessing that God has provided whereby we can come into His Presence. If we would take time to think through this, it will absolutely confound us. To think, the Creator of all things, God Himself, has told us to "come boldly to the throne of grace," into His very presence, and to bare our hearts, our praise, our burdens, our hurts, and our needs before Him. That is inconceivable, beyond our understanding; yet in His condescending love, this blessed privilege is ours! If we could in some measure comprehend the magnitude of this privilege of grace, it would transform our lives and empower us to be the effective "channel of blessing" God wants us to be.

What happens when we come before His Throne of Grace? We enter into the Sanctuary of God...the Secret Place of His Tabernacle...the Holy of Holies...WHERE GOD IS! It is where we relinquish all the strongholds of "self," cast ourselves upon His mercy, and experience the "infusion of His grace." It is there we recognize our "nothingness" and lay hold of His Mighty Power. It is the place of "quiet repose" where we sense His Holiness and find solace in His Rest.

At the Throne of Grace we learn to lean unreservedly upon Him, to be strength for our weakness, wisdom for our folly, love for our hatred, grace for our anger, freedom for our bondage, joy for our sorrow, and the anchor for our faith. It is where we pour out our hearts in praise and thanksgiving for our redemption. It is the hiding place where He meets us "as we are" in our need and desperation. It is where we hear Him say, "I will never leave you or forsake you; I am with you always."

At the Throne of Grace He reveals Himself anew and afresh unto us as the Mighty God, the Everlasting Father, the God of all Comfort, the Source of our Strength, the Good Shepherd, and the One who is "able to do exceeding abundantly above all we can ask or even imagine."

John Bunyan said, "In prayer, it is better to have a heart without words than words without a heart." His Throne of Grace is where we come with a "broken and contrite heart" that we may hear Him speak to us. Oh Lord, give us ears to hear, a receptive heart, and a spirit to respond to all that you want to say unto us, that we may be channels through which you can manifest your love and grace to all we encounter each day. We will not progress in our spiritual life any farther than we progress in prayer. We will never stand taller than when we are on our knees before God in fervent prayer.

Abounding Love and Patience in Persecutions

"We are bound to thank God always for you, that your faith grows exceedingly, the love of everyone of you all toward each other abounds, for your patience and faith in all your persecutions and tribulations that you endure."
2 Thessalonians 1:3, 4

These new Believers in Thessalonica were drawing deeply from the well of living water. Not only was their faith growing exceedingly, but they had abounding love, not only for God, but also toward each other. This is no less remarkable than their increasing faith. One spirit prevailed in the whole body of Believers. The time once spent in venting their differences and exercising their preferences was now spent in fervent prayer and intercession for one another. This solidified their faith and bonded their mutual affection to each other. Fervent prayer directed their attention and hearts toward the Lord and His Sufficiency rather than toward their prevailing petty circumstances. It was a bulwark to counteract the trials and persecutions they were encountering because of their faith in Christ. This demonstrated their progressive growth in grace: how they were being drawn together by the Holy Spirit, how they were being formed into the image of Christ, and how His love was making deep inroads into their daily lives. How blessed it is when the unity of the Spirit is perseveringly kept in the bond of peace. Then we see the Holy Spirit working freely and fully through Christians to accomplish His will, His plan, and His purpose.

We often wonder, "Why doesn't God move among us in His mighty power?" The answer is very simple; we are the problem! We need to change the focus of our lives to seek the Mind of Christ; to tear down the boundaries we impose on our spiritual lives; and to have open, receptive, and responsive hearts to the prompting of the Holy Spirit. Then with cleansed hearts and a contrite spirit, God can begin that work of grace we all need so desperately. We must start at the foot of the Cross.

These Believers also manifested invincible patience as they encountered cruel and bitter persecutions. Their trials and adversities had been severe, but their enemies did not intimidate them and the attacks of their foes did not discourage or devastate them. They held fast the "profession of their faith" without wavering. They "were in nothing terrified by their adversaries." They "had respect unto the recompense of the reward." They took joyfully the afflictions thrust upon them, knowing they had enough in heaven to compensate for it all. They "gloried in the Cross of Christ." They "rejoiced that they were counted worthy to bear it for His sake." In the midst of it all, "They possessed their souls in patience." Wow! What a tremendous testimony from new Christians who "dared to believe." They had a heart for God and a hunger to pursue their faith with purpose. Oh that we might find these life-changing qualities true and evident in our lives. What a radical change it would make in our Spiritual Journey, and what an impact we would make on our liberal self-seeking society.

People today are looking for a faith in God that is real. A faith that finds its way into our life and makes a transforming change in the way we live. True faith in Christ results in the virtues of Christ being lived through us by His Indwelling Presence. It is not I, but Christ! What a miracle of His grace, mercy, and love!

The Best Robe...a Ring... Shoes...the Fatted Calf

"But the father said to his servants, Bring forth the best robe, and put it on him; and put a ring on his hand, and shoes on his feet: And bring hither the fatted calf. For this my son was dead, and is alive again; he was lost, and is found." Luke 15:22-24

One of the most beautiful accounts of the "unconditional love of God" is revealed in the story of the "prodigal son" and his return to his father. I never read this without being strongly moved in my spirit by the "love and grace of the father" in receiving his son back home again. Why did the son leave such a place of security and love? Basically, he did not want to submit his will to the authority of his father, regardless of how loving and beneficent the father might have been. The "lure of sin," the urge to be independent, and the gratification of his lust for the pleasures of the world beguiled him. He thought that without restraint he would be free to order the course of his life. The chords of deceitfulness, initiated by Satan, entangled him. You are familiar with the awful consequences of his choice, but let me highlight a few of them:

- Choosing not to be ruled by God, he is compelled to serve Satan.

- Refusing to feed on the Bread of Life, he feeds on husks fed to the swine.
- Aspiring for the world to serve him, he becomes the slave of its bondage.
- Leaving a house of love, he dwells in the land of sin, hate, and rebellion.

Then, we read, "He came to himself." What do you think that means? Much could be said here, but let me say that he saw the wretchedness of his life and the consequences of his choice. Notice carefully that He realized first and foremost that he had sinned against God! He recognized his unworthiness and was willing to 'accept' the grace of his father. This is the core of his repentance. Now let's look at the father.

Was the father surprised by the son's return? No. I'm sure that every day the father looked down that empty road. But one day, HE SAW HIS SON! Can you imagine how he must have felt? And what was the father's attitude? Revenge, retaliation, reprimand? No, it was nothing short of UNCONDITIONAL LOVE, a heart of forgiveness, grace, mercy, and restoration! "Get the best robe, a ring, shoes, the fatted calf. My son has returned; he was lost but now is found!" There was great joy, and full and free pardon. Once again the son was given a seat at the father's table! How beautifully this scene resembles the fathomless love of God.

The depth of our sin, the wretchedness of our life, the extreme rebellion of our heart, when confronted and confessed unto HIM, "to whom we have sinned," only reveals the magnitude of God's unconditional Love and Grace. Deserving only His righteous judgment, He is ever standing with His arms spread wide, ready, willing, and anxious to receive, forgive, and reconcile us to the Father. We are fully restored, accepted in the Beloved, and given a seat at the FATHER'S TABLE! Oh the grace that is greater than all our sin. "Marvelous, matchless, infinite grace...grace that exceeds our sin and our guilt, freely bestowed on all who will believe." Have you experienced His matchless grace? Oh to know the joy and peace of resting in the arms of grace of our loving Lord.

Wise and Understanding

"Who is wise and understanding among you? Let him show it by his good life, by deeds done in the humility that comes from wisdom." James 3:13

James made it very clear in his epistle that we should demonstrate, in our walk and in our works, evident proof of what we proclaim in words as our faith, and what we believe. Wisdom differs from knowledge. All of us have seen a person who never had the opportunity for a formal education, but was endowed with an understanding heart that gave forth words of wisdom that often were astounding. Wisdom is not measured by the number of degrees accumulated, or by much learning, but by applying what one has learned in the deeds we do and knowing how to use what we have learned. This is applicable to our spiritual life as well. It is not a matter of acquiring truth from sermons or through much reading, but by applying truth to our daily walk that others might see truth demonstrated in the way we live, evident in our lifestyle.

God's wisdom is full of mercy and good fruits, without partiality and hypocrisy. It is sincere and open, steady and consistent, and ever seeking righteousness and peace. Our words and lifestyles reveal what is within our hearts, the true motive that prompts our thoughts and finds its way in the deeds we do. How imperative it is to live circumspectly before others a life that will glorify God. We must be on guard against the insidious ways of Satan to destroy our testimony and the effects of our lives on others. The application of Truth to our everyday practical life, empowered by the Holy Spirit, will have an everlasting impact on all we meet. Many Believers underestimate the need for a "pure heart and a right spirit" before God. Emphasis is put on the major concerns without regard for the "little foxes that spoil the vine." How many lives have been wrecked in a "moment of time" when they yielded to some fleshly desire, considered so trivial, but ultimately disastrous to them. We must be vigilant, steadfast, and sensitive to the Holy Spirit, who seeks to lead and protect us.

When English explorer Sir Francis Drake returned from his fifth voyage around the world, he was caught in a violent storm on the Thames River. As his vessel was tossed to and fro and appeared ready to run aground, the Old Mariner stood up, clinched his fist and shouted, "Can it be that I have braved the dangers of seven seas, have sailed through mighty storms, and must now come home to be drowned in a ditch?"

How insidious the enemy when he invades our lives unawares, infiltrates areas where we think we are strong, and, if left unchecked, causes our downfall. By relaxing our vigil and failing to heed the prompting of the Holy Spirit, Satan can make even the strongest person susceptible to fall. Often, our greatest danger does not occur in the heaving seas, but in the quiet, unsuspected waters where we are prone to be overconfident and careless! May the Lord give us a spirit that is sensitive to the invasive elements that seek to disrupt and defeat all that God desires for us to be. Only as we lean upon Him can we be triumphant and victorious.

Let Us Run the Race

"Wherefore seeing we also are compassed about with so great a cloud of witnesses, let us lay aside every weight, and the sin that doth so easily beset us, and let us run with patience the race that is set before us, looking unto Jesus the author and finisher of our faith." Hebrews 12:1, 2

*D*r. Bill Coker gives us some thoughts that are so applicable and heart-searching. Paul speaks of our spiritual journey as an athlete who is running a race. The Greek word for race is "agoon," from which we derive the word "agony." The idea is one of struggle, a contest, and a conflict. The Bible does not say, "If you will only believe, everything will be sunshine; no more sorrow, pain, or heartache; all will be easy." Rather, Paul says there is a race before us; a road paved with difficulty, conflict, struggle, adversity, and trial; and we are continually surrounded with battles. You will find the roadside strewn with fallen disciples who had good intentions but became casualties in the fight. The challenge is to "run with patience, with perseverance, with a steadfast faith in Christ." The hymn by Isaac Watts is one we should read again and again, asking the challenging questions:

"Am I a soldier of the Cross, a follower of the Lamb?
    And shall I fear to own His cause, or blush to speak His name?

Must I be carried to the skies, on flowery beds of ease,
    While others fought to win the prize, and sailed through
    bloody seas?
Are there no foes for me to face? Must I not stem the flood?
    Is this vile world a friend to grace, to help me on to God?
Sure I must fight, if I would reign; increase my courage, Lord.
    I'll bear the toil, endure the pain, supported by His Word!"

There are no prerequisites to be a disciple, but there are requisites to "run the race." There is Complete Commitment. "Lay aside every weight, every sin." Someone asked the late Bear Bryant, the ultra-successful head football coach at the University of Alabama, "What makes your players so determined to win?" His answer was simple, but one he had instilled into their hearts. He said, "Because there's nothing else." A winning attitude demands commitment to excellence.

On a flight from New York City to San Francisco, I was seated next to a 75-year-old Taiwanese man who ran in the 1936 Olympics. He was returning home, having just finished running in the Southeastern Masters Track Meet for Seniors in Raleigh, North Carolina. Then he showed me the three medals he had won: a Gold Medal for 3,000 meters, another Gold Medal for 1,500 meters, and a Silver Medal for 800 meters. I asked him, "How does a man your age train to endure such a challenge?" He said, "I get up at six every morning and run five miles. I've been doing that for 50 years! I have a commitment TO BE THE BEST! This is the focus of my athletic life. I must maintain a balanced diet, a structure of physical exercise, and a determination to run the race with one objective in mind, TO WIN. If I compromise in my discipline, I will simply be another runner, not a winner." I thought, how determined are we to be God's Best? How willing are we "to lay aside every weight, every sin, that doth so easily beset us, and run with patience [perseverance] the race that is set before us?" How can we? BY LOOKING UNTO JESUS, our consummate goal!

The Gift of God

"For by grace are you saved through faith, and that not of yourselves; it is the gift of God, not of works, lest any man should boost." Ephesians 2:8, 9

*M*any people are confused regarding God's gift of salvation and eternal life. Let's summarize man's scenario and see if this will help you to understand it better from God's perspective and from the Scriptures.

God gave Adam and Eve the wonderful quality of faith. There are two kinds of faith: natural faith and spiritual faith. The only difference is the "object to which that faith is exercised." They enjoyed spiritual faith when they communed and walked with God in the garden; peace, love, joy, contentment, and freedom. God also gave them "free will," the ability to choose and to make their own decisions. When they were beguiled by the serpent, they chose to disobey, and were immediately separated from God. For the first time, they were fearful and ashamed, and they hid from God. Their spiritual faith was lost, severed by their disobedience. Because of their sin, we received a sinful nature that is at enmity with God and has separated us from God. But God has provided a way whereby we can be reconciled unto Him.

Through His infinite condescending love, God sent His Son Jesus Christ to take our place in punishment. On Calvary's Cross, Christ paid the redeeming price for our sin. He shed His blood to satisfy the Justice of God regarding our sin. "He who knew no sin, was made sin for us, that we might be made the righteousness of God in Him." He died that we might live! But his redemption does not take place until we exercise saving faith in the "provision God has made through Jesus Christ." We are saved by God's grace. Faith is the vehicle through which we lay claim to what God has provided in Christ. Even the "faith to believe" is "not of ourselves; it is the gift of God."

God says "our righteousness" is as filthy rags. We cannot initiate redemption or reconciliation. God must do this. When Adam sinned, a great gulf was fixed between man in his sin and Eternal Life. There is no way man can bridge this chasm within himself. God has "bridged this gulf" so that man can get to the other side and be reconciled to Him. But the bridge can be crossed only "one way." At the entrance to the bridge, there is a CROSS. The Cross represents Jesus, who says, "I am the Way, the Truth, and the Life. No man comes to the Father but by me." The way has been provided. Faith to believe has been given to you. Your free will to choose must be exercised in response to the Holy Spirit awakening you to your sin. He is pointing you to God's ONLY PROVISION for your forgiveness and eternal salvation through His Son, the Lord Jesus Christ. God has done everything necessary for you to be saved. You must respond in faith, believing and accepting what He has provided. To accept Christ as your Lord and Saviour is to receive Eternal Life and be restored to full union and fellowship with God! "For God so loved the world that he gave his one and only Son, that whoever believes in him shall not perish but have eternal life." To reject Christ is to bear one day the awful judgment of God, which is Eternal Condemnation and Separation from God in the lake of fire. The choice is yours.

Holy Brethren

"Wherefore, holy brethren, partakers of the heavenly calling, consider the Apostle and High Priest of our profession, Christ Jesus." Hebrews 3:1

We all find it encouraging being in the "inner circle" or in a personal relationship with other people. There is a special sense of care and consideration, understanding and concern, when we are bonded together in such a fellowship. How beautifully Paul refers to these fellow Believers who have been bonded together by the love of God. He refers to them as "holy brethren," those who have been made "righteous" and have been brought into a "oneness of spirit" by the power of God. Their consecration to God and one another is very special, because they partake of the heavenly calling and share in God's plan and purpose for their lives. In sharing his calling, he says, "Attentively fix your thoughts on Jesus." Focus the intent of your life on the High Priest, whom we confessed to be ours when we embraced the Christian faith, the One who was faithful to God who appointed Him. What a blessed foundation for our friendship with others. He is the Pre-eminent One, the One who seals us together, and the One to whom we fix our hearts and will. What a difference this would make in our relationships with fellow Believers, if this were the basis of our bonding. We would "prefer others" more than ourselves.

Then Paul says, "Consider, attentively fix your thoughts on Jesus, our High Priest, who was faithful to the One who appointed Him." God sent Him to be our Saviour and the Lord of our life. He is the express image of God, the brightness of His glory, who upholds all things by the word of His power. But look at His life: "Fear the Lord, and serve him in truth with all your heart; for consider how great things he hath done for you." To contemplate the Lord Jesus in all of His Excellency and Glory should be the richest delight of our souls, and should compel us to unreserved obedience and commitment to Him.

Paul calls their attention to Christ, our High Priest. Do you ever pause to consider the important ministry that He is engaged in now for us? He is seated at the right hand of the Father, making intercession for us, pleading our cause. "For we have not a high priest which cannot be touched with the feelings of our infirmities; but was in all points tempted like as we are, yet without sin." He bids us to "come boldly to the throne of grace, that we may obtain mercy and find grace to help in time of need." He is our High Priest, our Advocate, and our Intercessor before God the Father. We will not receive any benefits from the "power" of His grace until we avail ourselves of the "provision" of His grace through prayer.

The whole work of redemption has been ordered of the Father and executed by the Son, and the Holy Spirit draws us unto Him. We must not stagger at any of the promises, but be strong and confident in faith, and give glory and praise to God. What a blessed "bond of love" is ours, as we share our heavenly calling with holy brethren, considering Him who gave Himself for us, that we might be reconciled to God! Hearts and lives bonded together, praying for one another, standing with one another, sharing our hurts and our victories, all because of the love, grace, and mercy of God! Praise the Lord!

Then Shall We Know

"Then shall we know, if we follow on to know the Lord: his going forth is prepared as the morning; and he shall come unto us as the rain, as the latter and former rain unto the earth." Hosea 6:3

The great objective of our heart should be TO KNOW CHRIST. The objective of our pursuit is not simply to have a speculative knowledge of Him. Many possess that knowledge and still have a heart as unsanctified as ever. But an experiential knowledge of Christ that comes from unremitting diligence in applying His Word in our practical, everyday lives, elevates us to a higher plane and intimacy with the Lord.

We come to know Christ by daring to trust Him in every area of our lives. To commit our walk to Him brings our lives into close union and abiding fellowship with Him. This abiding relationship results in a transforming knowledge of Christ. The Truth and Principles of His Word become the means by which our life is radically changed, and the Holy Spirit forms and shapes our lives to be conformed into His image. It is then that HIS LIFE LIVES through us and manifests righteousness and true holiness. As Paul testified, "I am crucified with Christ; nevertheless, it is not I that live, but Christ lives in me, and the life which I now live in the flesh I live by the faith of the Son of God."

This is not the work of a day, a month, or a year. It is a life-long commitment to become like Him. If we think we have arrived, that we have attained that level, and are already made perfect, we may rest assured that we have made little progress in our spiritual life. Paul, after preaching 20 years, still desired to "know Him more perfectly." He said, "I want to KNOW CHRIST and the power of His resurrection, and the fellowship of sharing in His sufferings, becoming like Him in His death and somehow to attain to the resurrection from the dead."

It's wonderful to have knowledge of God's Word, but to "experience His Word in our lives" gives us an assurance and blessing that is attained in no other way. To know promises of God's Word through memory is comforting, but to see that promise active and made real by experimental faith, makes His Word become alive and a vibrant part of our lives. To see the results of His interceding for us, going before us and preparing the way, to see Him work in and through us in things beyond our capabilities in answer to prayer, is to have a Living Faith, where Christ is a Living Reality in every phase of our life!

I know well my own sinfulness and failures, but I also know the virtue of His Blood. I know well my own weaknesses and vulnerability, but I also know the sufficiency of His Grace. I know well the deceitfulness and treachery of my heart, but I also know the surety of His promises. I know well the faulty ways of my walk, but I also know the "exceeding great and precious promises, that by these ye might be partakers of the divine nature." It is in this life of BECOMING that we begin to KNOW HIM in the wonder of His Majesty and Grace. What an exciting adventure awaits everyone who will DARE TO BELIEVE and will launch out into uncharted waters by faith. It is there we will "see His wonders in the deep."

Let This Mind Be in You

"Let this mind be in you, which was also in Christ Jesus."
Philippians 2:5

*W*hat drives your life? What motivates your decisions? What establishes your purpose? What solidifies the principles that you live by? A. W. Tozer, in his book *"The Pursuit of God,"* brings out so strongly that our sacrament (our covenant with God) should be evident in "all of our life," not just in our religious circles. God is involved in everything we do, and the life we live should be a "constant and consistent sacrament to God." Paul challenges the Believers at Philippi saying, "Let this mind be in you, which was also in Christ Jesus."

James questions the faith of Christians when it does not manifest itself in works. If what we believe does not relate and apply to our daily lives and manifest itself in all of our relations, he questions the genuineness of our faith. Paul says our lives are governed by one of two things: "They who are after the flesh do mind the things of the flesh [the mind of the flesh], and they that are after the Spirit do mind the things of the Spirit [the mind of the Spirit]."

When "the flesh" controls our minds, our lives will be subjected to and driven by selfish interests and desires, leading to a life filled with the shallow, superficial values of the world. Such a life is focused on self; therefore, the priorities and principles of our lives are limited to the boundaries of our own making. Such a life is not submissive to

God and is hostile to all things pertaining to God. We are without hope and without God, and ultimately we will receive the fruit of our life – eternal separation from God and eternal condemnation by God.

To be governed by the Spirit is to surrender our will to the Authority and Lordship of Christ, to have the "mind of Christ." He who created all things, and by whom all things exist and are held together, now governs and controls our life. The Holy Spirit now indwells our life and possesses us. When He filters into every phase of our life and activity, then we will know in reality what the Psalmist wrote: "You will show me the path of life: in your presence is fullness of joy, at your right hand there are pleasures forever-more." God will be pre-eminent in our life and magnified through our life. What drives your life? Who governs your life – the mind of the flesh or the mind of the Spirit? Oh to know the joy and peace of being "abandoned completely" unto God.

The Mind of Christ has a "defined direction" and a blessed eternal destiny. It "always causes us to triumph in Christ." "We are to God the aroma of Christ." He instills in us a compassion for people and gives unto us an understanding of His Word and a view of the bountiful riches of Christ. He gives unto us "exceeding great and precious promises, that by these we might be partakers of the divine nature." He empowers us to stand firmly in faithfulness to God! This is the incredible blessing and privilege we have as a child of God. Oh that we might maximize our life by simply being a "channel of blessing" by the power of the Holy Spirit. May the whole of our life be occupied by the fullness of the Holy Spirit, with the adequacy of Christ!

The Joy of the Lord

"Love does not delight in evil but rejoices with the truth."
1 Cor. 13: 6

*O*ne of the significant hallmarks of a Christian is the unique characteristic of joy. This joy springs from the presence of God in a person's life. It is not something we conjure up. We cannot produce joy; it comes from only one resource, God. It is often referred to as "the joy of the Lord" or "joy in the Holy Spirit." Nehemiah told Israel, "The joy of the Lord is your strength."

Joy is one of the grand attributes of God Himself. Often we find Believers who see God as an august, austere, awesome judge standing aloof and apart from us in the agony of our human anguish. God is the One who longs for us, searches for us, and, when we are found, reveals Himself unto us with unspeakable joy. He alone can give joy that is full of glory, thanksgiving, and praise unto the Lord of our life!

How does this differ from happiness? Joy and happiness spring from entirely different sources. Happiness is conditional and dependent upon what is occurring in our lives. It is bound up with the behavior of people, the sequence of events, or the circumstances we find ourselves in. Happiness is vulnerable, insecure, unreliable, and unpredictable. You say, "That's good, I'm happy, or that's bad, I'm unhappy." You can apply this to people, wealth, business, social interactions, possessions, or any other encounters.

Joy is founded upon and springs from God. David wrote, "Thou wilt show me the path of life; in thy presence is fullness of joy, at thy right hand are pleasures forevermore." Joy is not dependent upon people, circumstances, or the course of events, but upon our relationship with the Lord. It is our confidence in His faithfulness and care for us that solidifies our joy in the Lord. However crushing or exasperating our circumstances may be, HE IS THERE! He does all things well. He takes the broken things of our lives and makes something beautiful out of them for His glory. David said in the midst of all his enemies, "The Lord is my rock, my fortress, and my deliverer, my God, my strength, in whom I will trust, my buckler, and the horn of my salvation, and my high tower."

Joy does not depend upon my performance, but upon my relationship with Jesus Christ. It is in the process of pouring His Life into me that HIS JOY springs up from the stony, hard-packed soil of my soul. The joy of knowing He is at work in me and I am under His care. When we permit God, through the Holy Spirit, to pervade every aspect of our lives, we become engulfed and quickened in a new dynamic dimension, so that the whole of our being becomes alive to His indwelling presence!

To actually experience the control of Christ in our conversation and life, is to sense the Sovereignty of the Lord bringing order out of confusion, direction out of chaos, and joy out of despondency. Joy is being in harmony with Him in the whole of our lives. Do not look for joy; turn your eyes upon Jesus! Our joy is in Him. Our strength is in His ability to produce the joy. "In His Presence is fullness of joy and pleasures forevermore!"

He Arose and Followed Him

"As he walked along, he saw Levi the son of Alphaeus sitting at the tax collector's booth. 'Follow me,' Jesus told him, and Levi got up and followed him." Mark 2:14

*J*esus was in the beginning of His ministry, performing miracles of healing, and meeting the needs of the people, when He confronted Levi (Matthew) and said unto him, "Follow me." I'm sure Matthew had seen Christ minister to the people and saw in Him the "hope" that his heart longed for, the One sent from God. He immediately left his post, followed the Lord, and became one of His disciples. What does it mean to "follow Him, to be His disciple"?

Discipleship is built entirely on the supernatural grace of God. We think we have to do exceptional things for God. We do not. We have to be exceptional in the ordinary things, to be "holy" in difficult circumstances among difficult people. Jesus said, "I have chosen you." We can disobey His call, but we can't generate it. He supernaturally draws us to Himself by the Holy Spirit. But what qualifies a person to be a disciple? This perplexes many people. Actually, our nothingness! There's nothing within our being that qualifies us to be chosen by God to be His disciple.

Only coming as we are in complete dependence upon Him can God clothe us with His sufficiency. Why? That no flesh should glory in his presence. "It is because of him that you are in Christ Jesus, who has become for us wisdom from God, that is, our righteousness, holiness, and redemption." God is not interested in who we are, or what we have, or the gifts we possess. He who calls us to walk, to live, and to serve will also equip us in all things so that we may be fruitful in our service and glorify Him in our life. How quickly we forget that.

Saul is a good illustration of this. You can read Saul's attitude by what he says to Samuel: "The soldiers brought them from the Amalekites; they spared the best of the sheep and cattle to sacrifice to the Lord your God, but we totally destroyed the rest." Look closely at Saul's thinking. Saul called "good" what God condemned. He wanted to "sacrifice to God" that which God hated. Saul usurped the Authority and Sovereignty of God by doing it "his way." He disregarded God's command by inserting his own will. Samuel answered Saul, "Does the Lord delight in burnt offerings and sacrifices as much as obeying the voice of the Lord? To obey is better than sacrifice and to heed is better than the fat of rams." Obedience must take precedence in all of our actions.

Why do we insist on doing things our way? Because we do not want to submit our will to the control and authority of God. The last thing we want to "let go" is the control of our lives. Simple obedience is submission and surrender to His will. To be a disciple begins with the Lord being in control of ALL of our life. Someone has wisely said, "If Christ is not the Lord of all, He is not the Lord at all." It is not "natural" for us to surrender our will. That's why discipleship is "supernatural." It is the work of the Holy Spirit probing our hearts and drawing us unto Himself. Then melting and molding our lives, that we might be channels through which His Spirit can flow fully. Discipleship demands commitment, discernment, and dedication.

Set Your Heart and Soul to Seek the Lord

"Now set your heart and your soul to seek the Lord your God; arise therefore, and build ye the sanctuary of the Lord God." 1 Chronicles 22:19

*W*henever God leads or calls us to any task for Him, He will always equip us for the work. Whenever God has a great work to be done, He will raise up His instruments and qualify them for executing His will. He called Moses to lead Israel out of the bondage of Egypt. He appointed Joseph to make proper preparations for the seven years of drought in Egypt. He transformed Paul, when He was ready to gather unto Himself a people from the Gentile nations. Whatever the task, God has His "man" at the right place, at the right time, to accomplish His will.

It is beyond our comprehension how God, through David, made preparation for the building of the Temple. Even the place where the Temple was built is significant. It was on Mt. Moriah. That was where Abraham, under the direction of God, brought Isaac to offer him as a sacrifice to God, hundreds of years before. The Temple was to be like no other structure the world had known, in magnificence, splendour, grandeur, and glory. The gold and silver David gathered from his own wealth and from other subjects was in millions upon millions. The precious stones they used were immense. David specified the choice wood to be used. The expense today would be impossible.

One of the most remarkable features in the building of this magnificent Temple was that all the wood and stones were prepared at a distance from the site, brought to the place, and made to fit perfectly. So perfect was their unerring skill, during the seven years it took to build the Temple, that when they assembled the materials into the building, they didn't have to use an axe or a hammer. And the whole structure was completed without the smallest noise. (1 Kings 6:7) When David was old, he made Solomon King over Israel and gathered together the Levites, who numbered 38,000 men ages 30 and older. Now let your mind wonder at the magnificence of this Temple. "David said, 24,000 are to supervise the work of the Temple of the Lord and 6,000 are to be officials and judges. 4,000 are to be gatekeepers and 4,000 are to praise the Lord with the musical instruments I have provided for that purpose!" Can you imagine the magnitude of such a magnificent Temple?

Then David gives this great gathering of men the "foundation" for their efforts and objectives. "Now devote your heart and soul to seeking your God." After everything is put into place for the building, David turns to Solomon and says, "Solomon, my son, know thou the God of thy father, and serve him with a perfect heart and with a willing mind." This charge was given before princes and great men gathered for this solemn occasion. Notice that David did not say, "Know the God of Israel," but "Know the God of thy father." He wanted Solomon to recognize the Character of God in all His dealings with him, in mercy, grace, love, forgiveness, and longsuffering. Know Him in an intimate and endearing way. Seek Him as a Friend, your portion, and your eternal great reward. Let Him be Your God Forever. May David's challenge to Solomon be our challenge as we complete every task in the "temple" of His making.

He Hath Chosen Us in Him

"He hath chosen us in him before the foundation of the world, that we should be holy and without blame before him in love." Ephesians 1:4

*P*aul, in writing this epistle from a dark, damp Roman prison, is caught up in the "wonder of God's grace" in all that God has done for us in Christ, and what He is yet to do for us through Christ. He is consumed by the exceeding greatness of God!

God has manifested His power in two great works. First, God called the Universe into existence out of nothing. However incomprehensibly great Creation is, it is not God's greatest work. He has done something far greater, which reveals Him in a far higher light. His greatest masterwork is the Redemption of Man. From his sinful lost condition, without hope, and without God, He reconciled him unto Himself, enabling him to sit at the Father's Table in heavenly places and be accepted in the Beloved! This is beyond our understanding! We will never be able to comprehend the "magnitude of God's grace" until we are with Him in glory and "behold the Lamb of God that was slain for the sin of man."

He is ever the One who initiates our relationship with Him. It is not we who loved Him; it was He who first loved us. We did not draw near unto Him; it was He who drew us unto Himself. In this first verse, God emphasizes "He hath chosen us in Him!" Have you ever stopped to wonder at the tremendous depth of this truth? We have been brought nigh by the Blood of Christ, adopted into the Family of God, and made new creatures in Christ. On Communion Sunday, when we take the bread and the cup, it may seem a small and insignificant tradition to some, but the reality of that symbolism is the foundation of our Salvation, the very basis on which our redemption rests. Our minds will never grasp the full depth of so great a Salvation purchased through His Atoning Blood. Is it any wonder that we ascend to glorious heights when we sing some of the blessed hymns of old? Hymns such as "Amazing Grace, How Sweet the Sound, That Saved a Wretch Like Me." Or a chorus like, "I Will Praise Him, Praise the Lamb for Sinners Slain." Or "Oh the Blood of Jesus That Washes White as Snow." Feel the burden of Paul's heart as he prays for the Believers whom he loves so dearly. Let these words be his prayer for you.

"That he may grant you, according to the riches of his glory, to be strengthened with might by his Spirit in the inner man. That Christ may dwell in your hearts by faith, that ye, being rooted and grounded in love, may be able to comprehend with all saints, what is the breath, and length, and depth, and height and to know the love of Christ which passes knowledge, that ye might be filled with all the fullness of God. Now unto him that is able to do exceeding abundantly above all that we can ask or think, through the power that works in us." Oh that these words may be a reality in our lives!

HE HATH CHOSEN US! His infinite condescending Love is inconceivable. How true this blessed hymn, "Marvellous, matchless, wondrous grace of our loving Lord, Grace that exceeds our sin and our guilt! Look, there is flowing a crimson tide; whiter than snow you may be today!"

Seek Ye First the Kingdom of God

"But seek ye first the kingdom of God, and his righteousness; and all these things shall be added unto you." Matthew 6:33

*M*an struggles daily trying to adjust his priorities to enjoy life to the fullest and to take advantage of all that life has to offer. He expends his time and exhausts his energy pursuing goals that constantly elude him, that are beyond his reach, that are unrealistic. Or he simply becomes inundated with the frustration of it all. Our priorities have roots in our values. Our values play a significant role that determines the focus of our Spiritual Journey.

As never before, we are overwhelmed with advertising for products we do not need but "cannot possibly live without." Things and possessions rule our lives, consume our time, and rob us of the quality of life we let slip by. Our thinking is cluttered with having more of what we don't need. Our decisions are influenced by secular values focused on satisfying a selfish lifestyle, ever drawing us away from God. We become the victim of the world's system of materialism and greed and wind up living within the bondage of our own making. You say, "I'm not like that. I have my priorities and try to focus on them with much effort." Let me tell you about an experience I had not long ago:

Flying from California to New York, I was seated beside a well-to-do farmer who was anxious to let everyone know how successful he was and the vast amount of land he farmed. We were fairly high off the ground when he turned to me and said, "We are now flying over the 10,000 acres I own and farm." Then he said something very profound that surprised even him: "It doesn't look so big when you see it from here." His perspective on life was from ground level. God wants us to view life from HIS PERSPECTIVE.

All of these things are but "fuel for the fire" in God's sight. The proper perspective, when founded on the proper relationship with God, gives life its proper meaning, its proper fulfillment, its proper purpose, and its proper value. We covet what we don't need and probably won't use, trying to satisfy needs that those things cannot meet. Our deepest need, craved by our heart and soul, is a personal relationship with God that will set us free from sin and the bondage of things that bind us. This is found only in Jesus Christ when He is our Saviour and the Lord of our life. How few consider the sobering fact that life is short at best. Life is uncertain, we have no promise of tomorrow, and we are only a breath away from eternity.

With renewed purpose of heart, we should live each day to the maximum for His glory. We should buy up every opportunity He places in our path, seek to encourage and strengthen others, and be a blessing to everyone we meet. We should align our lives with the current of God's love and live each day with eternity's values in view. We have but one opportunity to make our life count for eternity. Don't abuse that gift with the encumbering fallacies of this world. Make God the priority of your life so that "out of your innermost being shall flow rivers of living water." Jesus said, "Seek ye first the kingdom of God and His righteousness, and all these things shall be added unto you."

Full of the Holy Ghost

"But he, being full of the Holy Ghost, looked up steadfastly into heaven, and saw the glory of God, and Jesus standing on the right hand of God." Acts 7:55

*O*ne of the great satisfactions in life is to have a profound impact upon someone's life that will have an eternal result. To see the radical transformation when Christ becomes their Saviour, to see them reach out to others in need, and to see God multiply the seed He has sown in their life.

Recently, friends of ours visited their daughter and son-in-law in another city. Their son-in-law had recently attended the Billy Graham Crusade and responded by receiving Jesus Christ as his Saviour. His goals and priorities took on new meaning, his attitude toward his wife and family was governed by a deeper love and concern, his whole life was radically changed, and he was anxious to attend and take part in the ministry of the church. A "spiritual transformation" had taken place by the power of God, which had an effect on "every phase of his life"! What he told his father-in-law was very special and meaningful. He said, "One of the reasons I accepted Christ as my Saviour was because of WHAT I SAW IN YOUR LIFE!" What a blessing and encouragement to the father-in-law. But that's what the "reality of Christ" is all about – making an impact on the lives of others. Was it anything he had done? No, it was the "Life of Christ living through him."

A committed life and a faithful witness, empowered by the Holy Spirit and placed in the Hands of God, will receive "eternal fruit" as God works in and through that life. It's not "who we are, what we have, or what we have accomplished"; it is the Holy Spirit fully possessing our life! How imperative it is to yield to His control and Lordship. The only thing that will count for eternity, as far as our lives are concerned, is WHAT GOD HAS DONE THROUGH US!

That's the difference between "profession" and "possession," between simply following tradition, custom, and a form of worship, and applying our faith to our lives. A life that is "possessed by His indwelling Holy Spirit" flows from within, expressing itself unto others. "Profession" denotes that the Truth has never "penetrated their hearts" or changed their lives. If our lives are going to impact others for Christ, the Truth of His Word must radically affect the way we live, before others and before God. Our faith must be applied to every phase of our lives. Christ died for us, that He might live in us and manifest His Life through us.

God's chosen vessels made an impact in their day. Look at the lives of Abraham, Moses, Joseph, Joshua, Gideon, Daniel, David, Elijah, John, Paul, Peter, and the countless pilgrims of the faith. They all made a difference in their day. WHY? Because they committed their lives without reservation unto God, "dared to believe," took God at His Word, and trusted Him fully. They were receptive to the Holy Spirit and responded to all He wanted to do in and through them. Let me ask you: "Is your life impacting others for Christ by the way you live, the things you say, and the commitment you have made?" Are you a candidate for all God wants to do in you? PUT GOD FIRST IN YOUR LIFE!

Be Renewed in the Spirit of Your Mind

"You were taught, with regard to your former way of life, to put off your old self, which is being corrupted by its deceitful desires; to be made new in the attitude of your mind; and to put on the new self, created to be like God in true righteousness and holiness. Ephesians 4:22-24

You can gauge the depth of a Christian's spiritual life by the things he puts first. Tell me his priorities and you tell me the focus of his life and his relationship with the Lord. Matthew said, "Wherefore by their fruits you will know them."

The voice from "the world" says, "Don't tell me how spiritual you are; show me by the way you live. Don't tell me how much you pray, show me the effect of prayer by the power of God being manifested in your daily walk. Don't tell me how much you read the Bible, show me how you have applied it by a righteous life and holy living. Don't tell me how much you love the Lord; show me how His love abounds in your life unto others. Don't tell me you are a Christian; show me the evidence through your godly character and committed life to Christ." They have had their full, and more, of superficial, shallow, uncommitted, ineffective religious professions. They are looking for and are influenced by a Christian whose life reveals a personal relationship with Christ and manifests the "fruit of the Spirit." And what is the fruit of the Spirit? It is "love, joy, peace, longsuffering, gentleness, goodness, faith, meekness, and temperance." Can these virtues be evidenced in our lives by our doing? Absolutely not! This "fruit" is initiated and manifested by the power of God living within the Believer. It is the manifestation of His indwelling Spirit in our lives. It's the result of being made a new creation in Christ, but there's more! Paul says, "Put off the old man and make no provision for the flesh; put on the new man, which after God is created in righteousness and true holiness."

The "old man" is what we are by birth, by nature, through inheritance, and by our actions. We are fallen, depraved, corrupt, sinful, and with a bias against God for evil. Our habits, associations, worldly interests, lifestyle, and our whole concept of life and God are from a "fallen nature." Therefore, Paul says, "Put off the old man." These things are incompatible with the "new man." Get rid of them! WHY? Because they belong to the sinful life of our past, the way we once lived.

What a radical difference in the way we were and the way God wants us to be! Paul knows what can happen when we "put off the old man and put on the new man". He's been there, done that, and his life was transformed from a persecutor of the Christians to an Apostle of Christ. He went from one end of the spectrum to the other. BUT SO CAN WE! When we yield the control of our lives to His Lordship, He clothes us with His Righteousness and Holiness! This is not our doing; IT IS GOD'S! Let us adorn our lives with the Fruit of the Spirit by the power of the Holy Spirit, being renewed daily in the spirit of our minds, and strengthened with His might by the Spirit in the inner man, that we may magnify Christ and impact lives for eternity. "Ye have not chosen me, but I have chosen you, and ordained you, that you should go and bring forth fruit."

The Song of the Lord Began

"He and all his men set out from Baalah of Judah to bring up from there the ark of God...They set the ark of God on a new cart." 2 Samuel 6:2, 3

*D*avid vowed, "I will allow no sleep to my eyes, no slumber to my eyelids, till I find a place for the Lord, a dwelling for the Mighty One of Israel." He was resolved to establish a "resting place" for the ark of God where Jehovah could be celebrated and worshipped. David acted with a full heart, with deep sincere longings after God, but his hopes were soon dashed to the ground. David had ignored the definite instructions about moving the ark. It was to be "carried upon the shoulders of the sons of Kohath," not on a new cart pulled by oxen. God's judgment fell upon Uzzah, when he sought to steady the ark and God smote him.

When David sought to move the ark of God, nothing is said of David "seeking the Lord." This was a very solemn and sacred occasion that must be observed by the explicit directions God had given. Should we wonder at what follows? If God's blessing is not sought, how can it be rightly expected? If prayer does not precede our best actions, what will they amount to? If, in any of our ways, God does not have "pre-eminence," we should not be surprised if they lead to disaster. David's desire was holy, his purpose was pure, his objective to honor God was proper, but he went about it in the "ways of man" rather than following the "precepts of God," and the results were devastating. It is not sufficient to have a worthy purpose and a proper spirit; the "work of God and our walk with God" must be done in "God's prescribed way." Anything other than that is but the expression of "self-will."

David realized that proper preparation must precede holy activities. Isaiah said. "Be ye clean that bare the vessels of the Lord." David is conscious of and acknowledges his past failures. "The Lord our God made a breach upon us for that we sought him not after due order." "And it was so, that when they that bare the ark had gone six paces, he sacrificed oxen and fatlings. And David danced before the Lord with all his might." Hezekiah had the same experience when he took the throne and immediately sought to cleanse the House of God. After everything was cleansed, repaired, and put in its proper place, "Hezekiah gave the order to sacrifice the burnt offering on the altar. As the sacrifice offering began, singing to the Lord began also, accompanied by trumpets."

How symbolic, how instructive, how true this scene. Before we can experience the Presence and Power of the Hand of God in our lives, we too must take our place, "identifying ourselves with the Lamb upon the altar," who was "made sin" for us, who today is the "burnt offering" that is sufficient for our cleansing and reconciliation. When self-will and sin are placed upon the altar and consumed by the cleansing fire of God, the "song of the Lord" will begin in our lives, resounding with the trumpets of God! Just prior to entering Jerusalem, David cried out, "Lift up your heads, O you gates, be lifted up, you ancient doors, that the King of glory may come in. Who is he, this King of Glory? The Lord Almighty, He is the King of Glory!"

Grow in Grace

"But grow in grace, and in the knowledge of our Lord and Saviour Jesus Christ." 2 Peter 3:18

One of the pitfalls Satan uses in the lives of many Christians, and especially new Christians, is to get them involved with spiritual activity in the ministry of the church. Now, many of these ministries are essential, and we should be active in them, but they are not to take precedence over our need for growing in grace. The problem comes when what we do is more important that what we are. The focus is on outward activity at the expense of inward spiritual growth. This results in having an abundance of Christians not grounded in the Truth. They accept concepts of truth without question, and follow without knowing why. They are satisfied with the status quo, no hunger for the Word, a shallow prayer life, and no roots of faith to hold them true and steadfast when adversity comes.

Peter challenges all Christians to grow in grace. You may say, "I go to church, tithe, am active in missions, and I'm even a Sunday school teacher. Am I not growing in grace?" My answer is, only if your relationship with the Lord is maturing, your prayer life is meaningful and consistent, you have a growing hunger to study the Scriptures and gain a greater knowledge of the Word, and you have compassion to reach out to others with your witness. When you yield unto Christ the will to control your life, then you begin to grow in grace. Our spiritual journey is one of becoming like Him. We never reach a point in our spiritual growth where we can say, "We have arrived." Our spiritual journey is a continual growing in faith and spiritual maturity.

Gary Collins, in his book *"The Soul Search,"* gives a wonderful spiritual exercise he goes through during his morning jog. His desire is to focus on Who God Is, the Greatness of God, the Nature of God, the Characteristics of God, What God is like, the Attributes of God, and much more. In his mind, he goes through the alphabet (except Q and Z). For each letter, he tries to thank God for WHO HE IS and WHAT HE IS LIKE. In this way, he expands his vision of the Greatness of God. Why don't you take a pen and paper and make your own list? Then get your concordance and begin a Bible study by looking up as many verses as you can on each thing you list. Your heart will "well up" in praise, adoration, and worship as you begin to realize the magnitude of WHO GOD IS! It will be exciting. You will begin to see what it means to grow in grace and in knowledge of our Lord Jesus Christ.

There is no shortcut to maturing in the faith, to developing an intimate relationship with the Lord that will radically change your life. The study of His Word is inexhaustible. You will never spend time that will be more rewarding or will enrich your life more! Jesus said, "Draw nigh unto me, and I will draw nigh unto you." Through communion with Him in Prayer, searching the Scriptures, walking in obedience, appropriating by faith His promises, and applying the Truth and Principles of the Scriptures to your everyday life, your spiritual journey will take on new life. You will begin the exciting adventure of "growing in grace and in knowledge of our Lord Jesus Christ."

I Will Rejoice in the Lord

"Though the fig tree does not bud and there are no grapes on the vines, though the olive crop fails and the fields produce no food, though there are no sheep in the pen and no cattle in the stalls, yet I will rejoice in the LORD, I will be joyful in God my Saviour. The Sovereign Lord is my strength; he makes my feet like the feet of a deer, and enables me to go on the heights." Habakkuk 3:17-19

This is one of the great testimonies in the Scriptures. Many of us have been in such distressing circumstances, have come to the end of our way, have exhausted every human resource, sought every option, consulted the wisdom of friends, then finally cast it all on the Lord. Then through prayer and waiting upon God, we saw His Mighty Hand meet us at the point of our need.

God knows the "boundary of our bewilderment," the limit to which we can go before we crash. God will proportion His strength unto us in relation to the depth of our need. When the trial comes and we get so low that there seems no way out but up, God will do one of two things: He will give us "deliverance from our trial" or He will give us "sufficient grace and strength to go through the trial victoriously." How encouraging are the words of Paul in 1 Corinthians 10:13: "No temptation |trial, adversity| has seized you except what is common to man. And God is faithful; he will not let you be tempted beyond what you can bear. But when you are tempted [tried], he will also provide a way out, so that you can stand up under it."

This was the testimony of Habakkuk. When he was bereft of all of the necessities of life – no resources to draw from, nowhere to turn for help, no hope for the future, humanly speaking – he said, "Yet I will rejoice in the Lord; I will be joyful in God my Saviour; the Sovereign Lord is my strength. He makes my feet like the feet of a deer." Wow! That is a constant, persevering, focused faith in an UNCHANGING ALL-SUFFCIENT GOD! Habakkuk realized that God could do all things. There was nothing beyond His power. No circumstances could overcome the plan and purpose of God in his life. He knew that God was with Him, regardless of his bewilderment. GOD IS ABLE IN THE TRIAL to triumphantly intercede for us. What is your faith focused upon? Upon your trying circumstances, or upon God, who is able to meet your every need?

How encouraging and applicable are the words of Isaiah 40:28-31: "Why do you say, O Jacob, and complain, O Israel, My way is hidden from the Lord and my cause is disregarded by my God? Do you not know? Have you not heard? The Lord is the everlasting God, the Creator of the ends of the earth. He will not grow tired or weary, and no one can fathom his understanding. He gives strength to the weary and increases the power of the weak. Even the youths grow tired and weary, and young men stumble and fall; but those who hope in the Lord will renew their strength. They will soar on wings like eagles; they shall run and not grow weary, they shall walk and not be faint." "You will keep in perfect peace him whose mind is steadfast, because he trusts in you. Trust in the Lord forever, for the Lord God is the Rock eternal."

For Me to Live Is Christ

"Christ shall be magnified in my body, whether it be by life, or by death. For me to live is Christ." Philippians 1:20, 21

The testimony of Ian Thomas could be the experience of so many who have yet to know the joy and reality of "Christ, who is our life." You say, "To the best of my knowledge, I am truthful with myself, to others, and to God. But there is something lacking in my life. I do not have the steadfast confidence that the indwelling life of Christ is the source of my strength, my power, my sufficiency, or life itself." At age 15, Ian Thomas dedicated his life to full-time service. For four years he was active in every Christian endeavour. He was planning to be a missionary to Africa and exerted his time and energy to the point of exhaustion. Yet he felt like a complete spiritual failure.

One night Thomas wept before God, confessing his utter failure. God focused his heart upon the message of "Christ, who is our life." The impact of Paul's testimony moved his heart: "For me to live is Christ." The words of Christ, "I am the way, the truth, and the life." Paul's admonition, "When Christ, who is our life, shall appear, then we shall be like him." It was as if God was saying, "You have been trying to live 'for' me the life I have been wanting to live 'through' you. It is Christ in you, the hope of glory." Your Peace, Joy, Victory, and Power are simply the "out-living of the in-living Christ"!

Dr. Raymond Edman, former president of Wheaton College, gave this analogy: "The secret is simple, yet it is profound. It is plain to have our heart fixed with faith and obedience, yet perplexing to our self-will and self-effort. The 'exchanged life' is an 'obtainment,' not an 'attainment.' It is a 'gift received,' not an 'achievement' to be earned. It is all from 'above', not from 'within us.' It's a life that 'arises out of death to ourselves,' not from any 'deeds we have done.' " What is the familiar pattern followed by so many who have experienced this glorious exchanged life?

First, there is agony of soul, an awareness of our need. The Holy Spirit makes clear to us our 'utter incapacity' to live this Christian life effectively and fruitfully, in our own strength. (Galatians 2:20) He is Lord of All.

Second, we follow in unreserved abandonment to Christ, "our members as instruments of righteousness unto God." (Romans 6:13) He is our Authority and Sovereign!

Third, there is an "appropriation by faith." The Holy Spirit fills the whole of our lives with the fullness of His presence and power. (Romans 12:2) He is our Life!

Fourth, we are to "abide in Christ." It is not striving or struggling, but resting in the Faithful One, receiving from Him our every need. (John 15:5) He is our Sufficiency!

Fifth, we are receiving from Him the life-giving waters from the Fountainhead of Life, that from "our innermost being shall flow rivers of living water." He is Our Resource!

There has to be a crucifixion before there can be a resurrection. You can't drive those nails into your hands; God has to do it. We want to hold on to our security, but it's hard to do so with those heavy spikes through our hands. You see, God demands that we let go of everything, IF HE IS TO BE OUR LIFE. To let go of our life is to gain His life in all its fullness, sufficiency, and glory!

Sanctify Yourselves

"Up, sanctify the people, and say, Sanctify yourselves against tomorrow; for thus saith the Lord God of Israel, There is an accursed thing in the midst of thee, O Israel; thou canst not stand before thine enemies, until ye take away the accursed thing from among you." Joshua 7:13

So often, when we have been successful at something, we forget how it was achieved. It could have been through hard, studious effort on our part; through determined perseverance; or through a set of circumstances that were very favourable for us. It still behooves us to "remember the pit from which we have been digged." In other words, don't be proud, boastful, and self-congratulatory. Remember where you came from, what you used to be, and how you started out. The people of Israel had this problem! They had just come from a miraculous victory at Jericho. At the command and under the direction and power of God, the walls of Jericho had fallen down, to the consternation of the enemy, which was defeated by the power of God! The Israelites were consumed by their victory and thought they were invincible. Their next foe was Ai, a small, seemingly insignificant village, and they said, "Let not all the men go up, for they of Ai are few." And what was the result? The "few" defeated them! "The hearts of the people melted and became as water." Israel was devastated. The people could not understand how they possibly could have been defeated.

Two things brought about the defeat. First, they underestimated the strength and power of the enemy. We have been there. We think it was "our" ingenuity, "our" cleverness, "our" wisdom, and "our" effort that brought about our progress and enabled us to achieve our measure of success! In reality, it was God who enabled us, who went before us and made the crooked ways straight. It was God who subdued the enemy and wrought the victory. How soon we forget "from whence we came."

Secondly, and the primary reason for Israel's defeat, was that there was "sin in the camp." Someone had disobeyed God. God had specifically told Joshua what they were to do. Notice God's response to their defeat. "Israel has sinned; they have violated my covenant, which I commanded them to keep. They have taken some of the devoted things; they have stolen, they have lied, they have put them with their own possessions. That is why the Israelites cannot stand against their enemies. I will not be with you anymore unless you destroy whatever among you is devoted to destruction." So it will be with us. The Lord will withhold His Hand from us when there is sin in our lives. God lays before us His requisites that are indispensable to His leading and working in our lives.

We must realize that it is only when our hearts and spirits are clean and pure before the Lord that we can expect His Hand upon us! We cannot condone sin, compromise our faith, or walk displeasing to the Lord and expect His blessing upon our life. David cried out, "Search me, O God, and know my heart: try me, and know my thoughts: and see if there be any wicked way in me, and lead me in the way everlasting." (Psalm 139:23, 24) It is with a contrite heart and a humble spirit that we should walk before God. Only then will the Holy Spirit flow freely and fully through us to the glory of the Father! May our hearts be ever sensitive, submissive, and responsive to His Spirit!

The Influence of a Life

"Set an example for the believers in speech, in life, in love, in faith, and in purity." 1 Timothy 4:12

As a Christian, it is of utmost importance to live "worthy of the Lord unto all." We never know how or who we influence through our life. A life that is anchored in the Word of God, whose roots are deeply planted in a faithful prayer life, whose heart is open to receive and respond to the Holy Spirit, whose life is motivated by the love of God, and whose walk reflects a life of praise and thanksgiving for all that God has done, will evidence the anointing of God's Presence and Power. God will use such a life to impact others as He lives through them.

God has placed you in a particular environment and circumstances, and has entrusted to you a ministry unto others. It is imperative that you have an ear to hear, a heart to receive, a spirit to respond to, and a life to live for the leading of the Holy Spirit. You are important to God. He has a specific ministry for you. He has given you a gift to be used for His glory. No one else can take your place in the plan and purpose God has for you. Paul said, "How then shall we live?"

Dr. V. Raymond Edman's booklet, *"How They Were Won,"* tells how John Wesley left England to be a missionary to the Indians of Georgia. Wesley later wrote, "I sought to convert the Indians, although I had not been so converted, although an Anglican Preacher." During a raging storm while crossing the Atlantic Ocean, he noticed a small group of Moravians calmly singing and praying, while others, including the ship's crew, were in dreadful fear. Conversation with the Moravians convinced him they steadfastly served the Lord in a manner wholly foreign to him. When John Wesley returned to England, he became a close friend of Peter Bohler, also a Moravian. Peter Bohler began to tell John Wesley of the deeper things of God and to instruct both John and his brother Charles Wesley in the Word of God, to which they had only an intellectual knowledge. Through the influence of Bohler's life and the teaching of the Word, both of them developed a personal relationship with Jesus Christ. Little did Peter Bohler know how far his committed life and faithfulness to God would reach!

John Wesley's life reads like fiction. He preached over 52,000 times and rode on horseback over 200,000 miles, preaching the Gospel in the hamlets of America. He became the instrument of God in one of the world's greatest revivals and founded the Methodist Church. He and Charles Wesley wrote over 1,000 hymns, such as *"Can It Be?"* ... *"O for a Thousand Tongues"* ... *"Hark, the Herald Angels Sing"* ... *"Jesus Lover of My Soul"* ... *"Take Time to be Holy"* ... *"Soldiers of Christ Arise"* ... and countless others. Lives of people around the world have been influenced through the ministry of John and Charles Wesley. It all started with the faithful witness of a few committed Moravians whose hearts were wholly given to the Lordship of Christ and who lived under the Sovereignty of God. Is your life an influence unto others of God's Saving Grace, of His Infinite Love and Mercy, of His Care and Compassion for you each day? Make Him the Lord of Your Life!

Treasures in Heaven

"But lay up for yourselves treasures in heaven, where neither moth nor rust doth corrupt, and where thieves do not break through and steal: for where your treasure is, there will your heart be also." Matthew 6:20, 21

What in life do you treasure most? What is your life centered on? What gives you the most satisfaction, joy, and fulfillment? What are the priorities of your life? Jesus gave the parable of the rich man who had great treasure. His barns were full and he made plans to build even-larger barns to hold the harvest of the coming year. Leaving God completely out of his life, he says, "And I will say to my soul, Soul, thou hast much goods laid up for many years; take thine ease, eat, drink, and be merry." But God said unto him, "Thou fool, this night thy soul shall be required of thee; then whose shall these things be, which thou hast provided?"

How descriptive this is of today. The rich man's folly was to count as his the things that might never come to him at all, and to reason 'within himself,' leaving God completely out of his life. The fulfillment of our lives must come "from without," not "from within" ourselves. The focus of our lives must be on what is in the realm outside ourselves; otherwise, it comes from within us and is stained with a self-centered motive and objective. Life, as God would have us know it, "consists not in the abundance of things a man possesses." Our deepest need is not food, clothing, and shelter.

IT IS GOD! Until this void is found in Jesus Christ, our hearts will ever be striving for things that will never fill this void and will be reaching for a treasure that constantly eludes us.

One of the wealthiest men who ever rose to power and influence in the British Empire was Cecil Rhodes. You might be familiar with the Rhodes Scholarships, given to exceptional students from around the world to study for two years at Oxford University in England. At age 27, Rhodes founded the De Beers Mining Co. in South Africa. Within eight short years, he controlled the diamond mining industry. Five years later, the gold mining industry was his. At age 36, he became Prime Minister of Cape Colony. He was so fabulously wealthy that, at his death, his legacy to the British Empire was the whole country of Rhodesia, equal in size to Germany, France, and Spain combined!

Perhaps one of the poorest, and yet one of the happiest men in England, was General William Booth, the founder of the Salvation Army. General Booth and Cecil Rhodes were well acquainted with each other. On one occasion General Booth asked Cecil Rhodes the striking question, "Mr. Rhodes, are you a happy man?" To which Rhodes replied, "Good heavens, no." What a contrast of two men with lives that were motivated and lived by opposite concerns. One was concerned with the accumulation of wealth fueled by self-centeredness. The other, by a heart controlled by God and a Life given to a World in great need!

Jesus said, "He that hath the Son hath life." Our fulfillment must be found OUTSIDE OURSELVES; it must be found in Christ. We are ever seeking to fulfill our desires and dreams within the realm of our own abilities, only to find that having gained them, our fulfillment eludes us. It is Christ, the giver of life, that will fill our void with an abundant life lived for others for our good and HIS GLORY!

From Within the Heart

"For from within, out of the heart of men, proceed evil thoughts... All these evil things come from within and defile the man." Mark 7:21, 22

*I*n our liberal society today, we find many theories, explanations, and excuses for man's behaviour. Except for those who believe and accept God's Word as the revelation of God, the standard by which we conduct ourselves, and the reason for our sinful behaviour and selfish ways, are only that man needs to have a more favourable environment. He simply needs to be better educated and should pull himself up by his own bootstraps. But the Bible says man is a "fallen creature," has a "sinful nature," is at enmity with God, and seeks to satisfy his corrupt nature by making SELF the center of his life.

In an address to the students at Asbury College, Dr. Peter Lord interrupted his message and asked one of the students to assist him. As the student stood beside him, he took a glass half filled with water and held it in his hand. He asked the student to grab his arm and violently shake it. Of course the water spilled out everywhere. Then he asked the students, "Why did that water spill out of the glass?" After they batted that around for a few minutes, they concluded that it spilled out of the glass because there was water in it. He then proceeded to explain that sin and all manner of corrupt things "erupt" from our lives because they are "within the heart of man." We do not become angry with others because they irritate us; they simply are the "occasion" that provokes our anger. The anger is already within our hearts; it just comes out when the occasion presents itself. It's the same with rebellion, resentment, bitterness, and all manner of sins that displease God. The only way we can control our behaviour is to recognize our need and then go to the One who can rectify that need, Jesus Christ, who is able to make us a "new creation" by His transforming power. (Ephesians 2:1-10 and 2 Corinthians 5:17)

Paul, addressing this need, said unto the Ephesian Christians, "Walk not as the Gentiles do." Who were they? They were the ones untouched by the Spirit of God, the non-believers. And how did they walk? What was their lifestyle? They walked in the vanity of their mind, in the futility of their own selfish desires, groping in despair, doing whatever pleased them, loving darkness rather than light. These are the characteristics of man "apart from God." Read Romans 1 for a picture of man's downward spiral, the result of rejecting God and pleasing himself. When Satan sears man's conscience, sin has no bounds. Satan is in control and leads man into every kind of impurity. Man becomes insensitive to God, his heart is hardened, and he opens up his life to the invasion of Satan and all of his devouring ways. Where is hope?

Isaiah said, "Let the wicked forsake his way, and the unrighteous man his thoughts; and let him return unto the Lord, and he will have mercy upon him, and to our God, for he shall abundantly pardon." Christ died "for" us, that He might live "in" us, to produce His life "through us." Jesus said, "I am the WAY, the TRUTH, and the LIFE. No man cometh unto the Father but by me."

Whatever You Have Seen in Me, Practice

"Whatever you have learned, or received, or heard from me, or seen in me, put into practice." Philippians 4:9

I have always been amazed at the things Paul said, but this verse causes me to nod my head in complete admiration. He says, "Look at all I've tried to teach you, given unto you, what you have heard me say, and the life I have lived. APPLY THESE THINGS TO YOUR LIFE!" Now that is quite a statement. I wonder if any of us could bare our life before others and say such a thing. I'm afraid not.

Throughout Paul's ministry, he was very conscious of setting an example before all the people he encountered of WHAT IT MEANS TO LIVE WHOLLY UNTO THE LORD. Look at Paul's attitude. He said, "I am a bond servant to everyone. Unto the Jews, I became as a Jew, that I might gain the Jews. To them that are under the law, I became as under the law. To them that are without the law, I became as one without the law. I am not without the law to God and lawless toward Him, but I am especially keeping within the law and have committed to the law of Christ, so that I may win those who are without law. To the weak, I have become weak, that I may win the weak. I have become all things to all men, that I might by all means [at all costs and in every way] save some [by winning them to faith in Jesus Christ]."

Paul was committed to the ministry God had entrusted to him. Even more, he was committed to God to be faithful and obedient to his calling. He wanted to live in such a way that the love of Christ would be magnified in and through his life and that his life would be a transparent testimony of his faith, consistent in his walk, sincere, and without hypocrisy. It is when people see the fruit of your faith that the witness of your faith is empowered by the Holy Spirit to penetrate the heart of an unbeliever.

The story is told of an unknown missionary laboring in the Philippines many years ago. Laboring in a predominantly Catholic country, where Protestant missionaries were not always appreciated, God laid on his heart a man by the name of Anacleto to witness of the saving grace of Christ. Anacleto, the father of eight children, was not receptive that he needed to be "born again" and shrugged off his friend time and again. But the missionary kept coming back, urging Anacleto to accept Christ as his Saviour. On the eleventh visit, Anacleto told him if he came back again he would kill him. Anacleto testified later, "When he came the twelfth time, I figured there must be something to this message, so I listened." It was then that Anacleto received Christ as Lord and Saviour. A missionary's faith was magnified by the way he lived, empowered by the Holy Spirit, and yielded eternal fruit. Today, Anacleto and his wife are in heaven, but all eight of their children are SERVING THE LORD as outstanding leaders in the Philippines and the United States. All are following in the footsteps of their father and mother and are DEVOTED TO GOD. Our responsibility is to be faithful and obedient. It is God's responsibility to bring forth the harvest. Your life may be the "only Gospel" others may ever know. LET CHRIST LIVE IN AND THROUGH YOU!

The Way of Man Is Not in Himself

"O Lord, I know that the way of man is not in himself: it is not in man that walketh to direct his steps." Jeremiah 10:23

*D*r. Dennis Kinlaw makes relevant man's point of reference. Man was made to produce and progress in life. We find man measuring almost everything, from "technical" space problems to "everyday" personality profiles and job performance. But here is the problem. If you are going to measure anything, you must have a frame of reference, a starting point. You cannot measure anything if the starting point moves, or if there is no starting point. Only when you have a stable starting point or a frame of reference can you measure anything.

Jeremiah recognized from the very beginning that any stable starting point or frame of reference would not be found within us; it is to be found somewhere else. If you call yourself the starting point, there will be no progress or productivity in your life. This is the essence of sin.

Man is so "focused in himself" that he becomes "his own frame of reference." His whole perspective of life, his identification with it, God, and His provision of love and grace are completely out of true meaning. How can you relate to the purpose of your being, the plan of God for your life, Eternity and all it holds forth, if you set up your "own" meaningless frame of reference?

That's why man has such a difficult time when he seeks to know what's right and what's wrong in everyday life. He uses his "own point of reference" and turns his back on the Lord, of whom it is said: He never changes; He's always there; He is the same yesterday, today, and forever. When I COME TO GOD, I have a frame of reference that is STEADFAST, STABLE, and ETERNAL. It's such folly for man to say, "I'm going to do it my way." Or to say, "It's my life; I'm going to live it the way I want to. Don't try to impose something foreign on me. I want to be myself." Man leaves God out of the equation of his life completely. The creature defying the Creator: How foolish!

The answer to man's need to know what's right is to "measure himself by the Standard of Truth, GOD'S WORD." His answer must be found in some ONE outside himself. The Scriptures never suggest that the answer to my needs is "within me," but it comes to me from ONE who is without, whose arms are ever open to receive me to Himself. He is ready to make that glorious exchange: my life for His Life, my way for His Way, my weakness for His Strength, my hopelessness for His Blessed Hope of Eternal Life.

The famous painting by Holman Hunt, *"The Light of the World,"* shows Jesus standing with a lantern in His hand waiting at the door. He is not standing in the middle of a man's life but on the "outside" knocking at the door, saying, "If any man will hear my voice and open the door, I will come in to him and sup with him and he with me." To many, He is still knocking at the door of their hearts. He wants to give them ETERNAL LIFE, a more abundant life that is beyond them, found ONLY IN JESUS. Have you opened the door of your heart and let Him in? He is knocking and waiting.

Love Must Be Sincere

"Love must be sincere. Hate what is evil; cling to what is good." Romans 12:9

Christianity's foundation is a Person, Jesus Christ. It is a life – His life lived through us. If the whole of our spiritual being is possessed by Jesus Christ, the life and love of Christ will be manifested in all that we do. Norman Grubb, that great man of faith, said, "It's not enough to be filled with the Holy Spirit; we need to be filled in an overflowing measure. It is the overflow of His Spirit that ministers and is a blessing, inspiration, and encouragement to others." What prevails above all else? God's love flowing freely and fully through us! Love should characterize the Believer who has become the "temple of the Holy Spirit." Love must take off every disguise of deceit, discharge every sham of shallowness, and cleanse every impediment that will hinder the flow of His love through us.

I was working on my sprinkler system, which had an ineffective sprinkler. The grass was brown from lack of water. I removed the sprinkler head and found a very small pebble lodged in the groove where the water sprays out. It was an impediment, ever so small, but it stopped the free flow of water. I thought, how true it is in my spiritual life when sin, ever so small, comes between my heart and the Holy Spirit. The flow of God's love through me ceases, and my spiritual life becomes ineffective and lifeless. Love must flow within our hearts unhindered, free from every impediment, with our lives made bare before God, overflowing with His life from within.

Can you think of someone who took a special interest in you and had a definite influence on your life? I recall the life of D. J. Fant. His life simply overflowed with the joy of the Lord and the presence of Christ. He had a real compassion for the lost and spent hours each day in prayer for ministries, pastors, friends, and missionaries around the world. Every day, beginning at 5 a.m., he was on his knees for the next three hours in prayer, interceding for others.

During his working days he was an engineer on the railroad. In front of his engine was a replica of an open Bible with the words "Jesus Saves." He preached in churches wherever his train would take him. He had tremendous influence on my life as one who was completely "sold out to God." God's love radiated through his life. Only eternity will tell of the multitudes he influenced with his simple, uneducated life that was steeped in the Word of God and filled to overflowing with His Spirit. His funeral was a time of "celebration" for one who had given so much to so many and glorified his blessed Lord. The influence of his life, lived under the control and Lordship of Christ, had an eternal impact on the lives of countless others.

What was the magnetic force that produced such startling results? It was a life without impediments, a life that was sincere and desirous of all God had for him. It was a transparent life in which the Holy Spirit filled his cup and the love of God compelled him to minister, encourage, challenge, and inspire others to give their lives to the Lord without reservation. Oh that we would put the "principles of our faith" into the "practice of our faith," letting HIS LIFE BE LIVED THROUGH US, WITHOUT ANY IMPEDIMENTS!

Substance...Hope...Evidence

"Now faith is being sure of what we hope for and certain of what we do not see." Hebrews 11:1

*F*aith does not rest upon promises. It rests in the One who has made the promise. Faith is the "whereby" that the just live by. It is a divine, supernatural, justifying, saving faith, the faith of God's elect. It is not of us; it is the operation of God, whereby all Believers are endowed from above. Faith gives the "things hoped for" a real substance, as if they were already present. Faith, being the "evidence of things not seen," is the means of the preservation for Believers against all opposition, under the fiercest of persecutions. It is faith that lifts us "above" our circumstances while we are yet "in" them. It enables us to live with things that are future and invisible. It gives sustenance to the Believer and provides evidence of the truth and reality that will secure him from falling, whatever the trial may be. When we exercise faith, claiming a promise God has given unto us, we are putting our confidence, trust, and reliance in the "infallible character of God" and the merits of His Son, Jesus Christ!

If I were to make a will, and if the day came when it was read, and if it said, "I leave to my daughter, Beverly, my ocean-going yacht; to Sharon, my French villa; and to Robin, my oil rights in Texas," they would say, "Dad really went off the deep end before he died, because he never had any of those things!" Such a will has no character and is absolutely meaningless. However, if a rich man dies, everyone pays very close attention to the reading of the will, because he has the "character, ability, and resources" to back what he has written.

Some years ago, a friend of mine commuted each week to New York City. About 50 miles north, the train would stop in the little town of Harmon, New York. He asked the conductor on one occasion, "Why are we stopping here?" "Oh, we switch engines here. We're not allowed to bring a steam engine into the city, so we're switching to an electric engine." When the conductor showed him the engine that would soon be attached to the train, my friend exclaimed, "You don't mean that little thing is going to pull this long train!" The conductor said, "No problem." He explained that there was a third rail along the tracks to which the "shoe" of the engine connected, supplying the power. With that, the train started forward, ever so smoothly, all the way to New York City. When they arrived, the conductor leaned over to my friend and said, "We made it, didn't we? You see, when that electric engine connected to the third rail, all the power generated from Niagara Falls was at its disposal." It's not the size of the engine that counts, but the SOURCE OF POWER to which it is connected. The "shoe" was the conduit. There was no power in the "shoe." It simply acted in "faith" and connected to the unlimited source of power from Niagara Falls. Let me ask you: Is your "shoe" in place? Are you connected by faith to His Infinite Power? It will take you safely all the way home. Remember, it's not the size of the engine that counts, but the Source of Power that determines our journey. Get Connected to His Power Plant! "The Lord is the strength of my life; of whom shall I be afraid?"

Conformed or Transformed?

"And be not conformed to this world: but be ye transformed by the renewing of your mind, that ye might prove what is that good, and acceptable, and perfect, will of God." Romans 12:2

*P*aul has presented in the first 11 chapters of Romans the deplorable condition of man, who is lost, without hope, without God, and the victim of his own sinful choices. God made provision for his sin through Christ, and reconciliation with God through His grace. In Chapter 12, he says, because of all that Christ has done for you, and in you, the most reasonable thing you can do is to "present your bodies a living sacrifice unto God." But how can we do this? Paul makes it very clear.

"Be not conformed to this world." What does he mean by that? Simply, don't be conformed to its systems, squeezed into its mold, and fashioned after or confined to its pattern or superficial customs. Don't be engulfed with the evaluations and priorities that the world places on "things." Many things put us in bondage when Satan infiltrates into our lives, deceives our thinking, and controls our attitudes. We become victims of worldly schemes that are under his control. This world has as its main goals fortune, fame, power, and pleasure. The problem with these goals is that "man makes them the consuming objects of his life." His life comes under their control and is corrupted by their influence. The goals that he is pursuing cannot satisfy the deep longing of his soul, or glorify God, when He is not the foremost priority. "There is a way which seems right unto man, but the end thereof are the ways of death." (Proverbs 14:12)

Paul says, "But be ye transformed by the renewing of your mind." Now, how can we be transformed? How can we have a renewed mind? Certainly not by anything "we" can do. We cannot achieve nor generate a radical change from one nature and life to another. This is solely the work of the Holy Spirit. It is for us to respond to the Spirit's probing and awakening us to the surrender of our will to His Lordship. Then, as we yield our lives to His control, respond to His leading, and live day by day in submission to His will, He begins the process of "conforming us to the image of His Son." Romans 6:29

The "renewing" of our minds and the "transforming" of our lives are elements in "becoming" like Christ. And what is the purpose for such a life? It is to be conformed to His image. He has saved us "that we may prove what is that good, and acceptable, and perfect, will of God." And how can we do this? By letting CHRIST RULE ON THE THRONE OF OUR LIFE! He wants to live His Life through us. Paul said, "Let this mind be in you which was also in Christ Jesus." What was the mind of Christ? It was complete submission to the will of the Father. It is when our entire thinking process takes on a new perspective. We no longer think within the boundaries of pleasing ourselves, but we are wholly desirous of pleasing the Lord. When He is the Sovereign of our lives, He will renew our minds, transform our lives, and control the process of conforming our lives to the image of His Son so "that we may prove what is that good, and acceptable, and perfect, will of God"!

Canaan Was All God Said It Was... But

"We went into the land to which you sent us, and it does flow with milk and honey! Here is its fruit. But the people who live there are powerful, and the cities are fortified and very large." Numbers 13:27, 28

We often stand on the very brink of God's blessing yet fail miserably to receive it. The people of Israel were led out of bondage in Egypt. All of Canaan was before them: the land God promised to Abraham, the land that flowed with milk and honey. All they had to do was "possess what God had already provided."

Moses calls the most "valiant" man from each tribe to him. He sends these 12 men to spy on the land and bring him a report. Now these were no ordinary men. They were men of proven courage, strength, and valour, the 12 "Best Men," one from each tribe.

Ten mighty men said, "It is all God said it was, BUT." They saw only the difficulties: the powerful people, giants compared to them; impregnable walled cities; and an unhealthy climate that ate up its inhabitants. They saw everything BUT GOD! Does that sound familiar to us today? They looked within themselves to their own strength. They acknowledged the difficulties, but denied that God was leading them. Everything before them was limited to the boundaries of their self-centered vision. They had lost sight of God, forgotten the promises of God, and had no faith to enter the land God had promised to them. Giant-like men, fortified cities: God had conquered it all for them!

Two humble men of God said, "He will lead us into that land and give it to us. Only do not rebel against the Lord. And do not be afraid of the people of the land, because we will swallow them up. Their protection is gone, but the Lord is with us. Do not be afraid of them." They recognized God had "brought them out of Egypt to bring them into Canaan," the land of promise. The people are mighty, but God is Mightier. Their fortifications are strong, but they cannot withstand God. They fight with the arm of the flesh; we fight with the arm of the Living God. No matter how numerous and powerful they are, they are only "bread for us." God is with us!

Faith looks to God and leaves out every discouraging circumstance. Faith looks outside of us and dares to trust God for the impossible, that which is beyond our capabilities. Let us go up, "not to conquer" the enemy, but to POSSESS what God has already conquered for us. The battle is over, the victory is ours, the food is prepared for us, and we have only to eat it! Whenever God leads us, He will equip and enable us for the task. However formidable the enemy, God is able to subdue, defeat, and destroy him and be our Sufficiency. Sometimes it takes years of struggling before we learn "at Jordan" what we should have learned "at the Red Sea" – GOD'S FAITHFULNESS and HIS MIGHTY POWER. Neither the wilderness nor Jordan was in God's plan for Israel. I wonder how many alarming circumstances we "create for ourselves" which never were in God's plan for us? God said, "Everywhere the sole of your foot treads upon is yours." Israel only possessed 25 percent of all the land God promised to them, unclaimed through unbelief! Oh that we might "possess our possessions" and appropriate all He has purchased for us!

Sow to Yourselves in Righteousness

"Sow to yourselves in righteousness, reap in mercy; break up your fallow ground: for it is time to seek the Lord, till he come and rain righteousness upon you." Hosea 10:12

$\mathcal{T}$he message from God through his prophet Hosea was God's steadfast and righteous love for His people. Repeatedly, God manifested His Love through His care and concern, through His provision and protection, through His grace and mercy, seeking to "draw them unto Himself" so they could know Him as their Everlasting Father and their Mighty God. He uses discipline to turn them from their sin, direct them in His way, and train them in the behaviour glorifying unto Him. The punishment was not to "give them what they deserve," but to lead them from their "destructive pursuit" to a "constructive alliance" with Him, free from their self-imposed bondage. This is precisely the Lord's intention in disciplining us today. It proves His Divine Love for us. The motive for His discipline is for "our good and His glory."

What happens when we embrace His discipline with a receptive and responsive spirit? What changes take place in our lives? Let me list just a few. It results in a cleansing of our hearts and a freedom and liberty of Spirit. It leads to restoration, reconciliation, and the warmth of His Love and abiding presence. It causes us to adjust our priorities and clearly focus our vision. We become an instrument of righteousness and a channel of blessing. We develop a defined direction of our way according to His way. Our faith becomes anchored in the Truth, and our life is made steadfast. The purpose of our pursuit becomes the expression of His leading.

"Our fathers disciplined us for a little while as they thought best, but God disciplines us for our good, that we may share in his holiness. No discipline seems pleasant at the time, but painful. Later, however, it produces a harvest of righteousness and peace for those who have been trained or exercised thereby." The discipline is only effective with those who are receptive and responsive to its intended purpose.

Michael Green, in his book "*1500 Illustrations for Biblical Preaching*," gives an experience of Andrew Murray, who was suffering terrible pain in his back. While eating breakfast, his hostess told him of a lady downstairs who was in great trouble and asked his advice for her. Andrew Murray handed her a piece of paper on which he had been writing and said, "Give her this advice I have written for myself; it may be that she will find it helpful." He had written, "First, God brought me here. It is by His Will I am in this place. In that I will rest. Next, He will keep me here in His Love and give me grace in this trial to behave as His child. Then say, He will make this trial a blessing, teaching me lessons He intends me to learn, and working in me the grace He means to bestow. And lastly say, In His good time, He can bring me out again. How and when, He knows. Therefore say, I am here by God's appointment, in His keeping, under His training, for His time; therefore I will praise His Name." "STAND STILL and see the salvation of the Lord."... "BE STILL and know that I am God."... "WAIT ON THE LORD, and He shall strengthen thine heart." May we "bend our hearts" to the plan and purpose of His will each day!

But God Is Faithful

"There hath no temptation taken you but such as is common to man: but God is faithful, who will not suffer you to be tempted above that ye are able; but will with the temptation also make a way to escape, that ye may be able to bear it."
1 Corinthians 10:13

God knows our lives. He is very conscious of our weaknesses and our strengths, and He has promised not to allow trials to come to us that are not common to everyone, but will "in" the trial be our sufficiency, strength, and comfort to carry us through. I'm sure you have often wondered, "Lord, why has this come upon me?"

The other day we had our piano tuned, and I was fascinated watching the piano tuner. The first thing he did was to activate his tuning fork, which was the "true standard pitch" by which all of the notes were to be measured. He struck the first note, then again, and again, until the piano was adjusted to correspond exactly to the pitch of the tuning fork. I thought he would never stop hitting those notes! He went through the entire keyboard, making every note correspond in its true pitch. I thought, Lord, the trials that you allow us to go through are like that piano. You are trying to align our lives with your will, plan, and purpose, but so many notes are out of tune. The Lord has to keep "banging away" at our lives to bring them to the "true standard" of His will.

Trials are also needed to "stretch" our faith, to drive our stakes of faith deep with confident trust in Christ, and to challenge us to walk in unwavering obedience. You might say, "I really don't need those trials. I can trust the Lord without them." The truth is, when our way is always smooth, we begin to rely upon "our resources" and finally think, "I can handle this; I'm doing pretty well on my own, and I really don't need the Lord." Paul tells us, "For whom the Lord loves, He chastens, and scourges every son he receives." Therefore, our adversities and trials come with plan and purpose. Notice carefully that it is "in" the trial that God makes a way of escape. (1 Corinthians 10:13)

"Moses drew near unto the thick darkness where God was." (Exodus 20:21) It is "in all these things we are more than conquerors through him that loved us." (Romans 8:37) It was "in" the many adversities and trials that Paul suffered and endured, that he learned to be content. It was "in" his weakness that he was made strong; it was when there was "no way out" and God said unto him, "My grace is sufficient for thee." What wonderful words of assurance and comfort He gives us in this verse: "But GOD IS FAITHFUL, who will IN the trial make a way of escape."

We grow in faith and maturity when we go through the trial with Christ, rather than being delivered from the trial by Christ. In His time, In His way, He perfects His will, and will be our Sufficiency! God is never too late nor does He ever come with too little. There are no circumstances that are beyond God's power and there is nothing too trivial for His love. DARE TO BELIEVE GOD "IN" THE TRIAL. HE IS FAITHFUL TO HIS OWN! "I Will Never Leave Thee or Forsake Thee!"

The Words of Amos

"The words of Amos, who was among the herdsmen of Tekoa, which he saw concerning Israel." Amos 1:1

Throughout the Scriptures, God brings forth His "mighty men" from the unknown, the uneducated, the ordinary, the fishermen, the shepherds, and from many walks of life that are not in the forefront of society, to accomplish unbelievable tasks and proclaim His message of Truth. Amos was just such a man – a simple herdsman, a master shepherd, and a tender of sycamore fruit. God reached out to the hills of the shepherd and spoke to Amos. He had a message from God to man.

As God so often did, He found a shepherd in obscurity. He chose Abraham to "father" the Nation of Israel. He chose Moses as he was attending his flock on the backside of the desert in Midian, to lead the children of Israel out of Egyptian bondage to Canaan. He reached out to the pasture of Bethlehem and found David to be Israel's greatest king. He found Joseph abandoned in a pit by his brothers and caused him to rise second only to the King of Egypt, for the salvation of that nation and his family. Gideon, Jeremiah, Daniel, Isaiah, John, Peter, Paul, and scores of others were used in miraculous ways as God came upon them in His mighty power.

You might say, "Well, that was back in the days of the prophets, during Biblical days. We don't see that kind of man today." But oh we do! Just years ago, the world was rocked by Martin Luther, John

Calvin, St. Augustine, John Huss, Hugh Latimer, John Wycliff, and countless others. Then along came John Bunyan, Francis of Assisi, John Wesley, Francis Asbury, and an array of dedicated missionaries, such as Hudson Taylor, David Livingston, John Goforth, C. T. Studd, and the five martyred missionaries to Ecuador. And don't forget the flaming evangelists, such as D. L. Moody, Charles Finney, George Whitefield, Billy Graham, and more.

What is so special about these "chosen vessels" of God? They were all "nobodies" until their hearts were "set aflame by God" and they dedicated their lives to the Lord without reservation. God empowered them with the Holy Spirit and used them to move the world for God. God gave them a vision and a life beyond themselves!

God is looking for a life that will "dare to believe" what HE CAN DO through one who is wholly committed unto Him. It's not what we have to offer Christ, but what He has to offer us. He is looking for the servant willing to be used of Him, where he is. Our responsibility is to be faithful, obedient, and prayerful, and to persevere with a sensitive, receptive spirit to the leading of the Holy Spirit. The results are God's responsibility. Eternal fruit is the result of His working through us. You are important to God! He has a plan and purpose for your life. He will equip you for every ministry He calls you to do. Seek His will, find your place of service, and pursue with perseverance all that God wants to do in and through your life. He will faithfully lead you and empower you!

So Walk in Him

"As ye have received Christ Jesus the Lord, so walk ye in Him." Colossians 2:6

*W*hat do you think "Practical Biblical Faith" is as it apples to our daily lives? Practical Biblical Faith in Christ means that we find the meaning of our life in Christ. He is the focal point of who I am, where I'm going, what I'm about, what my purpose is, and what my goals are. All of these are tied to the fact of my being in Christ. Faith in Christ means that Jesus Christ is the center of my belief in life and myself. He is the One who shapes, directs, and controls my life. He is the Lord of my life and is in sovereign control.

Don Fletcher, in his book on Faith, gave this definition: "Faith is a radical commitment of the whole person to the Living Christ, a commitment that entails knowledge, trust, and obedience." Let me ask you: Do you find the meaning of your life through your relationship to Jesus Christ? Is He simply an appendage to your life, unnecessary to the daily routine of your life? Or do you believe in Him to the extent that you are under the constraint of the One to whom, by faith, you have committed your life? Practical Biblical Faith is having Jesus Christ as the Object of our Faith, when our faith becomes so significant and convincing that we cannot but believe. It is then that Paul's admonition "to so walk in Him" becomes the hallmark of our Spiritual Journey. We walk in continual dependence on the Lord Jesus Christ for all we stand in need of, incorporating Christ into every phase of our life. And what do we need in order to walk circumspectly before others? Grace to sanctify and renew us every day, wisdom, discernment, strength, peace, love, comfort, encouragement, direction, knowledge of His will, the consciousness of His Presence, and many other attributes of our blessed Lord.

So how do we make all of this become a reality in our life? In 1 John 2:6 we read, "He that abides in Him ought himself also to walk, even as He walked." We are to abide in Him even as the "branch abides in the vine." That implies incessantly deriving our strength and nourishment from the Lord, from His Word, and from our communion with Him in prayer. We will begin our walk with the Lord in His glorious companionship.

To so walk necessitates our commitment to a life of holiness. This means being set apart unto the Lord, separated unto His will, His Word, His Way. It involves not only the removal of sin and evil from our lives, the "putting off of the old man," but also the positive cultivation of "putting on the new man, which, after God, is created in righteousness and true holiness." We are to be "renewed in the spirit of our mind."

God's desire for us in our walk is to be "conformed unto the image of His Son." Being submissive to the Holy Spirit in all things. God so molds our lives and effectively changes our perspectives, priorities, and attitudes that we begin to manifest the fruit of the Spirit in our daily walk. As God has sovereign control of our lives, the Holy Spirit does the supernatural transforming work of grace. Our walk will then "be a living sacrifice, holy, acceptable unto God which is our reasonable service." And we will "prove what is that good, and acceptable, and perfect, will of God."

God Remembers... We Forget

"And thou shalt remember all the way which the Lord thy God led thee these forty years in the wilderness, to humble thee, and to prove thee, to know what was in thine heart, whether thou wouldest keep his commandments, or no."
Deuteronomy 8:2

How characteristic it was of the people of Israel, after they had been so miraculously delivered from the bondage and slavery of Egypt, to focus their hearts upon themselves and forget so quickly the mercy and grace of God, instead of delighting themselves in the goodness of God. How soon we forget and are consumed with our interests and concerns.

An unrest and discontent swept through the people of Israel that resulted in their desire to have a King "like the other nations." They wanted a King to lead them in their battles, to rule and reign over them, someone visible that they could proclaim as their exalted King. But their desires were rooted in something that was much deeper. It was the ancient sin, the desire to be "ruled by man rather than God", a prideful rejection of God's way and will, and a determination to be governed as they thought best. We want to do it "our way." Man does not want to surrender the "authority he possesses over his will" to the Sovereignty of God. How quickly they "forgot" they were "God's Chosen People". God had made a covenant with them, that if they would obey His commandments and follow His way, His hand of blessing and power would be upon them. He would be their God and they His people.

We FORGET WHAT GOD REMEMBERS. How quickly we forget His care, protection, leading, provision, compassion, love, grace, mercy, longsuffering, sufficiency, and all the multitude of benefits we have in Him. We forget what God remembers.

We REMEMBER WHAT GOD FORGETS. We cannot stand in His holy presence without being aware of our abominable sins and wretchedness, our unworthiness, our rebellion and abounding sin. But God said, "I will remove your sins as far as the east is from the west; I will remember them no more. Though your sins be as scarlet, they shall be white as snow; though they be red like crimson, they shall be as wool."

The magnitude of God's infinite grace is beyond our comprehension. There are awesome dangers when we persist in doing it our way, regardless of the consequences that lurk in the shadows. When we choose to do what we want, rather than yielding to God's way and will, He does not take away our freedom to choose. However, neither does He take away the consequences of our choice. God will not impose His Will or His way on us. After repeated complaining and rebellion by the people of Israel, we read, "He gave them their request, but sent leanness into their soul."

Are you a "slave to your self-imposed bondage" that inflicts a costly price now and in eternity, or a "bond-servant of Christ" who knows how to direct our paths and order our way? Oh the joy, peace, and liberty of being "set free". Free from the entanglement and bondage of being under the control of the enemy of our soul. Satan cleverly disguises his methods and objective of bringing us into such a state of frustration and confusion that our eyes are blinded to the Truth, and we resist the prompting of the Holy Spirit to reveal Satan's insidious ways to us. God desires that we live in the liberty and freedom of His presence and power. Remember God's Faithfulness.

The Lord Looked Upon Peter

"And the Lord turned, and looked upon Peter. And Peter remembered the word of the Lord, how he had said unto him, before the cock crow, you shall deny me thrice. And Peter went out, and wept bitterly." Luke 22:61, 62

This is one of the most solemn accounts in the Scriptures. I'm sure this scene was forever ingrained upon the heart of Peter. He would never forget his betrayal in the palace courtyard, when Jesus turned and looked upon him. Can you imagine being Peter at that moment? Only hours before, Peter had boasted that he would never deny Christ, even if he had to pay with his life. He would stand true beside his Lord. Now, only hours after his intimate meeting when the Lord washed the disciples' feet, Peter is accused by a lowly maid. He falls miserably and denies being one of His disciples.

What was in that look that pierced the heart and soul of this disciple? Can you imagine how penetrating, convicting, and revealing those eyes must have been as the Lord looked upon Peter? Did those eyes of Jesus reveal anger, disgust or revenge? No! His eyes were filled with Divine compassion, pity, and love for one who had miserably fallen. His eyes revealed infinite mercy and grace that melted the denying heart of Peter. The "look of Christ" brought penetrating conviction that awakened Peter to his dreadful denial. Christ's "heart of love" drove Peter to his knees in bitter repentance that soon brought reconciliation.

Like Peter, many have fallen unmercifully to the depths of sin and despair. Many are critical and quickly point their finger at this fallen disciple, but few have wept bitterly in heart-wrenching repentance as Peter did. The remembrance of his fall never left him, but he saw more. He saw the fathomless love of God, the love that flowed at Calvary, the infinite grace that forgave him in his darkest hour and restored him unto Christ.

Deep are the wounds of many lives that have been abused, neglected, unloved, and forgotten by those closest to them. How needful it is for Christians to come alongside of those who are starving for acceptance and understanding. The Good Samaritan, when he saw the beaten and needy stranger beside the road, "went where he was" and not only ministered to his wounds but found a place for him to stay. He told the owner to tend to any of his needs and he would pay for the service. What's so significant? The Good Samaritan "identified with the stranger in his need." How we need to do the same. Whether people are in destitute conditions or in disarming circumstances, they need someone to come alongside of them and identify with them, seek to minister to their needs, encourage and pray with them. Our testimony is not established "in the church", but out in the byways of life where we encounter people with broken hearts, facing adversities and trials that are tearing their lives apart. We need to manifest the "love of God" unto them and put our compassion and faith into action, showing a cynical, unbelieving world the "reality of a Christ-centred life." It is then that their lives will be impacted with the Gospel and the walls of defiance and unbelief will crumble. What the world "sees" in your life means much more than what you "say" with your lips. Demonstrate His grace, mercy, and love by the life you live and the compassion of your heart! "And the Lord turned and looked upon Peter, and Peter remembered."

I Come to You in the Name of the Lord

"Thou comest to me with a sword, and with a spear, and with a shield: but I come to thee in the name of the Lord of hosts, the God of the armies of Israel, whom you have defied." 1 Samuel 17:45

The secret of David's victory was what he had learned in the fields as a shepherd tending his sheep. It was there that David had been taught the wondrous resources which are in God through faith. Numerous times he had to defend and protect his sheep, and there was no one to help but God. He had slain the bear and had slain the lion. HOW? He trusted God to be his strength and a resource for all his needs. In the quietness of the hills of Bethlehem, David's patience was tried and tested, his faith stretched and strengthened, and his pride replaced with humility, and he learned to focus his life steadfastly on the Lord. One of Saul's servants says, "Behold, I have seen a son of Jesse the Bethlehemite, that is cunning in playing, and a mighty valiant man, and a man of war, and prudent in matters, and a comely person, and the Lord is with him."

The dominant characteristic in David's life was his unfeigned and unsurpassed devotion to God, His Word, and His will. God "teaches in secret" the soul that He has chosen to walk before others in the glorious might of His Power. Walking with God, spending time with Him in the "secret place of the Most High", David found the "Key to his Confidence"... the "Source of His Strength"... and the "Certainty of His Victory." He tells Saul, "The battle is the Lord's!" He went forth as an instrument in the Hand of God. There was no doubt in David's mind as to the outcome, because "God had gone before and prepared the way."

God often uses our very trial to make us strong in faith and to instill our hearts with renewed confidence in His faithfulness. Our extremities are "occasions" God places in our way to prove His Sufficiency. God does not always, nor generally, act immediately when we are "pressed by the enemy" or find ourselves in some trying adversity. In Isaiah 30:15, we read, He "waits to be gracious unto us." Why? That we may more fully recognize our "utter help-lessness"' and realize our need to trust Him completely. That His gracious Hand of Deliverance may be seen more clearly and His merciful interceding for us be appreciated more fully. It is "only through Him" we have victory.

All seemed to be lost; sure defeat was imminent. When no one from Saul's army would step forward, GOD HAD HIS MAN! In "God's Time," David stepped forward and vindicated the glorious Name of Jehovah! God is never too late, nor does He ever come with too little. "Greater is He that is in you than he that is in the world." God gave victory to David, so that "all the assembly might know, that God saves not with sword or spear but by the Word of His Power." It is well for us to remember, "The Battle is the Lord's", but He has given us the "armor" to engage the enemy. Girded with Truth, the Breastplate of Righteousness. Shod with the Gospel, the Shield of Faith, the Helmet of Salvation, the Sword of the Spirit, and THE WORD OF GOD...we go forward in confident trust in our Mighty God!

The Man That Trusts in the Lord

"Cursed be the man that trusteth in man, and maketh flesh his arm, and whose heart departeth from the Lord... Blessed is the man that trusteth in the Lord, and whose hope the Lord is." Jeremiah 17:5, 7

*C*hicago has the world's largest display of original artifacts from the RMS TITANIC. A large, tarnished brass bell is suspended from the ceiling of a dark room. It sets a sombre tone and is a striking symbol of the tragedy that took place in the North Atlantic on April 14, 1912. Sadly, the officers of the Titanic ignored the warnings of four ships that were in the icy waters, confident of their ship and their ability to cruise through danger. The Titanic had lifeboats to accommodate only one-third of its passengers. The lack of adequate lifeboats testified to the misconceptions and false security that convinced the leaders that the Titanic was UNSINKABLE.

It is ironic that a cartoon appeared showing the sinking Titanic in the background and a picture of Wall Street. The caption speaks so clearly of the liberal, freewheeling lifestyle of many today. It said, "Even God Can't Sink This Ship!" My immediate reaction was, Oh how easily God can bring about the destruction of any security man may devise! How deceived man is to think that billions of dollars secured in investments on Wall Street can avert for a second the

Mighty Hand of God. If your security in not in the infinite Grace of God, YOU HAVE NO SECURITY! Fragile, unstable, and fallible are the ways of man. God says, "Cursed is the man that trusts in man."

God said unto Israel, "I have set before you, life and death, blessings and cursing, now choose life, so that your children may live and that you may love the Lord your God, listen to his voice, and hold fast to him. For the Lord is your life."

God is saying the same today. The choice is yours. Many of our problems and difficulties are the result of our choices. You say, "I didn't choose all these things that have happened to me that have almost taken my life." I say, "God set before you a choice, life or death, blessings or curses. Did you do what God said and choose life? Did you choose to love the Lord, to listen to His voice, to hold fast to Him?" "Well, no, I made my own decision and I chose to go the way I thought best." Then you are now reaping the consequences of "your choice" of turning your back on God and going your own way. The decisions we make determine the direction we take and the consequences we can expect.

Rick Warren, in his book *"The Purpose Driven Life,"* made this striking observation: "Without God, life has no purpose, and without purpose, life has no meaning. Without meaning, life has no significance or hope." Our culture today presses us to such a fast pace that we do not heed God's words, "Be still, and know that I am God." Take time to evaluate your life in the light of eternity, in the light of what God says in His Word. "There is a way which seemeth right unto man, but the end thereof are the ways of death." Jesus said, "I am the WAY...the TRUTH...and the LIFE. No man cometh unto the Father but by me." Is your hope, security, even life itself, found in Christ? He's the ONLY WAY!

The Word Came the Second Time

"And the word of the Lord came unto Jonah the second time. Arise and go unto Nineveh, that great city, and preach unto it the preaching that I bid thee." Jonah 3:1, 2

How typical Jonah is of our self-directed ways. Having heard God's command to go to Nineveh, he turns to his own way and goes in another direction. The amazing thing is that God speaks to him a second time. How long-suffering God was to Jonah, and also to us today, when we persist on "going our way" instead of yielding in obedience to God's way, thinking we know best and can certainly handle our lives without Him. Jeremiah said. "O Lord, I know that the way of man is not in himself: it is not in man that walketh to direct his steps."

Have you ever noticed that "reconciliation" always begins with God? He is the One that seeks us. We did not seek Him; He sought us. We did not love Him; He first loved us. We did not draw ourselves unto Him; He draws us unto the Father. So often when we face a decision of obedience, we start rationalizing; we weigh the pros and cons, and we doubt and debate issues. We would save ourselves many heart-wrenching experiences if we would follow in "simple obedience."

Obedience and faith go hand-in-hand. Obedience often means we have to "step out in faith" when we do not see anything. Obedience to my notion means we clear the ground first by our intelligence, rely upon our cautious calculations, and make a decision from our own evaluation. Faith is not intelligent understanding; it's more than that. Faith is a deliberate commitment to God, a trust in the faithful character of God, when I do not see a way. It is complete reliance on and trust in the One who is true, able, and faithful to "perfect that which concerns us." It is when we place our complete confidence in God, and if He does not come through for us, we're done!

Another important factor in obedience is our "immediate response." When God told Abraham to take his only son, the son he loved, and offer him for a burnt offering, we read, "Abraham rose up early" and made his way to follow the Lord's leading. The simplicity of Abraham's response exemplifies his "complete trust in God." His immediate obedience reflects his sense of urgency in following God's will in the most trying time of his life. God said, "Take thy son," not presently, not when it's convenient, not when you come to some decision, but NOW.

To climb the heights that God wants to take us to, we cannot have a passive attitude toward God. God wants immediate, full, and complete response, exercised in an obedience that stems from a heart of love for Him. Abraham did not yield to his own sympathies, his own insights, his own reasoning, or "anything" that would compete with or hinder his complete obedience to God.

God wants to lead us into ventures of faith to a "life that is beyond ourselves." He wants to take us into experiences that can only be accomplished by the manifestation of His mighty power in our lives! He has a plan and a purpose for our lives that is "exceeding abundantly above all we can ask or even think." Are you a candidate for such a life, an exciting adventure of faith for His glory? "He is faithful who has called you!"

That You Might Have Life

"I am come that they might have life, and that they might
have it more abundantly." John 10:10

As a Christian, how would you describe an "abundant life"?
You have experienced the "new birth" and have received
the indwelling of His Life in you, but what did Jesus mean when He
said, "that they may have life more abundantly?" I think the majority of Christians would say: the blessing of being saved from the
penalty of their sins, having access to the benefits of His grace, the
assurance of eternal life by His grace, the blessed hope of eternal
life, or the opportunity of serving Him. These are great blessings
to us, and most Christians rejoice in these benefits of His grace, but
I'm afraid that the majority of Christians respond to these blessings
in a spirit of detached formalism. They adhere to, but do not apply,
the Truth to their lives.

They attend services, sing, pray, read the Bible, and are active in
some type of ministry, because they feel obligated as a member of
the church. They give of their means, because they feel required to
do so, regardless of the amount they give. Their spiritual lives seem
to result from following a pattern laid out for them by the church.
Form, tradition, ceremony, and custom seem to take precedence over
a "life transformed by the Holy Spirit." Walking in the path of life
that evidences His Presence and Power living in and through them

everyday, being subject in all things to His Authority, and living under the joy of His Lordship all are foreign to them.

Jasher Heifetz, the world-renowned violinist, described the difference between one who plays a "fiddle" and one who plays a "violin." He said the fiddler plays musical notes. The violinist interprets the notes and the spirit of the composer from his soul, and the result is beautiful music. It's the same in our spiritual life. God wants to make active in our daily lives the "intent and spirit of the Master Composer." This cannot be done by simply "following a form of godliness and denying the power thereof." It is when we open our hearts to be filled to overflowing with HIS LIFE, surrendering our "worn-out instrument" into the Hands of His Masterful Artistry. HE will transform the redundant notes of our life into an Abundant Life in Christ. Then, and only then, will we know what it truly means to be "IN CHRIST."

On July 6, 1947, life took on a new meaning for me. I stood before our pastor and exchanged wedding vows with my soon-to-be wife. He said to me, "Do you take Millie...etc?" and I said, "I do." "Will you be...etc?" and I said, "I will." And she responded the same. Life completely changed for both of us. The past was gone. All that was yet to be was now established as the "beginning." The Abundant Life before us depended upon our love for each other expressed in a yielding to each other, preferring the other rather than oneself, and having Christ as the Authority of our lives. The result has been an intimate relationship that bonded our lives together in His Love and in a blessed marriage that has lasted for 56 years. Why? Because we have a self-giving love, seeking to please each other. So, in our spiritual journey, Christ must have pre-eminence in All Things. WHEN HE IS LORD, HE GIVES UNTO US AN ABUNDANT LIFE!

This is the Way ... Walk Ye in it

"And thine ears shall hear a word behind thee, saying, This is the way, walk ye in it, when ye turn to the right hand, and when ye turn to the left." Isaiah 30:21

In the very beginning of Creation, God set forth His terms whereby He would dwell with man. It was on the basis of man honoring God for WHO HE IS. When God established His Covenant with His people Israel, the terms were to "obey His Commandments and walk in His Law." God spoke again and again unto Israel, basically saying, "If you obey my voice and walk in my way, I will pour out my blessings upon you." But, "They soon forgot his works; they waited not for his counsel, but lusted exceedingly in the wilderness and tempted God in the desert. And he gave them their request, but sent leanness into their soul." Such are the ways of man, refusing to be subject to the "Authority of God", insisting on his way and his will, and rejecting God's way of blessing.

Had they simply walked in obedience to God, they would have entered into an "intimate relationship" with God that would have been beyond their comprehension. They would have experienced the Glory of His Presence, the Might of His Power, the Companionship of His Grace, and the exceeding Wonders of His Love.

We are faced with a major problem today that affects the whole of our Spiritual Journey. The average Christian has little, if any, concept of the Majesty of God. The "right concept of God" is essential and basic to our spiritual walk. What would you say if I asked, "WHO IS GOD?" or "WHAT IS GOD LIKE?"

A. W. Tozer, in "The *Attributes of God*," had these penetrating words to say about the Majesty of God: "When we try to imagine what God is like, we must of necessity use 'that which is not like God' as a raw material for our minds to work on. Hence, whatever we visualize God to be, He Is Not, for we have constructed our image out of that which He has made, and what He has made is not God. If we insist upon trying to imagine God, we end up with an "idol" made not with hands but with thought. An idol of the mind is as offensive to God as an idol of the hand. God's essential nature is INCOMPREHENSIBLE."

You might say, "What does all of that have to do with me and my Spiritual Journey?" It has everything to do with it. Our "concept of God" will determine the Depth of our Commitment – How great is God? The Intimacy of our Relationship with God – How much does He deserve our love? The Steadfastness of our Faith – Is He able to hold us secure in all the encounters of life? The Foundation of our Faith – Upon what is our spiritual life built? God in His Holiness, Righteousness, and Justice, along with His Love, Grace, and Mercy, must be the "point of reference" on which our lives must be founded, sustained, and lived. When we recognize the "greatness of God," we will realize the encompassing need to humbly bow before Him with a "broken heart and a contrite spirit," even as David did, and stand in awe of ALL HE IS! It is only then that we will hear Him say, "This is the way; walk ye in it." But how Glorious!

The Race that Is Set Before Us

"Let us run with patience the race that is set before us, looking unto Jesus, the author and finisher of our faith." Hebrews 12:1, 2

The Jewish Believers were going through a great deal of difficulty, including many trying experiences; things did not immediately go well with them. They often found themselves separated from loved ones, stoned, threatened, persecuted, and ostracized from society. It caused them to ask, "Why should we follow Jesus anyway? After all, we had so much going for us before we believed and followed Him. Why should we pay this kind of price and suffer these kinds of things, just to identify with this movement and align ourselves with this man Jesus?"

In Hebrews 11, He gives examples of many "heroes of the faith," whose lives were characterized by FAITH amidst unbelievable suffering and hardships. He gives the challenge to every Believer: "Wherefore, seeing we are compassed about with so great a cloud of witnesses, let us lay aside every weight, and the sin which doth so easily beset us, and let us run with patience the race that is set before us, LOOKING UNTO JESUS." Dr. Bill Coker gives some penetrating thoughts regarding the race that we run in our Spiritual Journey.

What a beautiful passage, because it reminds us of things we should never forget. One of the reasons I love and appreciate the Bible and my faith in Jesus Christ is, that it is a REALISTIC FAITH and a REALISTIC WORD. The writer compares our life to a race that will not be easy; there is a struggle to be engaged in with those of different values. There is a conflict with the evil ways of Satan, and we will face a continual challenge to our priorities. Adversities will be on every hand. It is a road paved with difficulty. But that is what Discipleship is all about. Life is a "battle" and you have to make a choice. Discipleship means entering the battle on behalf of the Gospel of Jesus Christ, by taking our place and engaging the enemy in the Resources and Sufficiency of Christ! We need to concentrate on the "steadfastness" of our race, rather than on the "swiftness" of our run. The first step "costs," but the last step "counts." Our eyes need to be fixed steadfastly, "looking unto Jesus" with complete confidence and unwavering faith, with patience and perseverance.

I was watching the Pepsi 400 stock car race at Daytona International Speedway recently, and I was strikingly impressed with what Jeff Gordon, one of the top stock car drivers, had on his dashboard. It was one word in large letters: PATIENCE! So many variables occur during the course of a race that can put a driver out of contention, but the one who drives with patience and perseveres with purpose often is the one who gets a break and surges ahead, gets the checkered flag, and crosses the finish line the winner!

Where in the world would we ever get "unwavering confidence" apart from Jesus? We cannot look to preachers, for preachers fail. Certainly, we should never look at each other for we are so undependable. There's only ONE to whom we can look, the ONE whose LIFE never varies, the ONE who never fails, the ONE who never changes, the ONE who is the same yesterday, today, and forever, JESUS CHRIST OUR LORD, the Author and Finisher of our faith! Turn your eyes upon Jesus with Steadfast Trust! "Let us run with patience the race that is set before us, looking unto Jesus."

When They Had Prayed

"And when they had prayed, the place was shaken where they were assembled together; and they were all filled with the Holy Ghost, and they spoke the Word of God with boldness." Acts 4:31

*G*od was preparing these disciples to preach the Gospel and establish the church. Before them was a road of difficulties, trials, abuse, false accusations, imprisonment, and beatings. How encouraging it is to see how they submitted to the Authority, Purpose, and Plan of God. They could not have gone through all they encountered in their own strength. God had prepared their hearts by "empowering them with the Holy Spirit" and giving them strength for every situation they faced. Prayer preceded their witness and walk. "And when they had prayed, the place was shaken where they were assembled together; and they were all filled with the Holy Ghost, and they spoke the Word with boldness." Four elements are evident in these early Believers:

First, there was a UNITY OF SPIRIT. Rejoicing in what God had done, they were "bonded together in a unity of spirit" they had never experienced before. Yet before them were experiences that would solidify their bonding even more: persecution, adversity, and trial. These encounters not only bonded them in unity, but also deepened their mutual love of Christ. The Holy Spirit will abound in us, in proportion as we possess the grace of God. Christian character is engrained into our lives through adversities.

Secondly, there was their GENEROSITY. They separated themselves from their own interests for the collective benefit of the whole assembly. Their concern and giving to one another was so great that their adversaries were compelled to say, "Behold, how these Christians love one another." When Christ reigns in our hearts, there will be an "unselfish and hilarious giving of ourselves" one to another.

Third, there was a POWERFUL WITNESS. These young converts saw the attitude manifested by the disciples after being reprimanded and beaten: They were "rejoicing that they had been counted worthy to suffer for His Name." No anger, resentment, bitterness, or retaliation, but rejoicing to be counted worthy. They recognized that the faith and love of these Christians was real. I want my life to be so committed and to embrace such a love of Christ!

Fourth, there was an AWARENESS OF GOD'S GRACE. They had a consciousness of the Presence and Power of God in their midst, an awareness of His matchless grace, mercy, and love. No wonder they had no problem seeing, hearing, and knowing the "mind of Christ", or experiencing such a display of His power through them.

"Be followers of them, who through faith and patience, now inherit the promises."

The PRINCIPLE from which they acted was governed by a supreme love of Christ.

They gave themselves unreservedly to the Lordship of Christ. STEADFAST OBEDIENCE to that principle governed their path of duty. They suffered in their witness for Christ, but rejoiced to be counted worthy. Christ was the motive of their actions and the object of their life. The MANNER in which they endured, good for evil, blessing for cursing, grace for anger, prayer for persecution, love for hate, was evident that Christ was SOVEREIGN and the LORD OF THEIR LIVES!

Walk in the Spirit

"If we live in the Spirit, let us also walk in the Spirit."
Galatians 5:25

*T*here are two covenants mentioned in the Epistle to the Galatians. One is the covenant of "works," and the other is the covenant of "grace." All mankind is under one covenant or the other. Those under the "covenant of works" are transgressors and are under the curse of God. The principle that rules their lives is called "the flesh," and all of its diabolical fruit is known as the "works of the flesh." These are mentioned by Paul in Galatians 5:19-21, with the conclusion that "they which do such things shall not inherit the kingdom of God."

You might say, "Well, how does one make the transition from the covenant of works to the covenant of grace?" It is by God's grace through faith in Jesus Christ as our Sin Bearer who paid the debt of our sin on Calvary's Cross. We accept Him as our personal Saviour, having taken the place we justly desired. God makes us "a new creation in Christ." The vital principle that now rules our life is known as the Spirit of Grace.

Someone has asked, "How can we recognize which principle people are living under?" It is by the fruit they bear. The fruit of their life displays the nature of its origin. A corrupt nature manifests abominable fruit that adorns those who are controlled by Satan. Paul said, "Be not deceived; God is not mocked: for whatsoever a man soweth, that shall he also reap. For he that soweth to his flesh shall of the flesh reap corruption."

What a contrast to the Believer who is under the covenant of grace and the influence of the Holy Spirit. John said, "Ye have not chosen me, but I have chosen you and ordained you, that you should go and bring forth fruit, and that your fruit should remain." Now what is this "fruit" that is of the Spirit? Paul says, "But the fruit of the Spirit is love, joy, peace, long-suffering, gentleness, goodness, faith, meekness, temperance: against such there is no law."

The first fruit that is mentioned is love, which is the foundation of our faith, the very essence of God, for God is Love. His love finds expression to the degree that God lives in and through our lives. The "fruit of the spirit" is bestowed only and always through the increased presence of His Person in our lives. The more I have of Christ, the more I have of His Love. The more I have of God, the more I have of His Goodness. The more I have of the Holy Spirit, the more I have of His Holiness. The love of God is the "Life of God" poured out lavishly and constantly. Only when our lives are in harmony with the love of God can we know the "will of God." Then the minute details of our life bear enormous meaning and purpose.

Everything must find its beginning and foundation in the Love of God if our lives are to be effective and fruitful for eternity. As the Holy Spirit controls our lives, so will we walk in the Spirit and reflect through our lives the "fruit" that only He can produce for His glory. Oh that we might be channels through which His Life can flow freely and fully! Is this the desire of your heart? What kind of fruit is your life bearing? Make Him the Lord and Sovereign of your life.

The Little Foxes That Ruin the Vineyard

"Catch for us the little foxes that ruin the vineyards, our vineyards that are in bloom." Song of Solomon 2:15

What would you say if I were to ask you, "When are we the most vulnerable to the infiltrating ways of Satan to disrupt, defeat, and destroy us?" I'm sure many would say, "when I'm lonely, physically weak, discouraged, or when someone that is my friend has mistreated me." Many of these times and more are valid when we are prime targets for Satan. But the most susceptible time is when we have just experienced our greatest victory. You might say, "Well, I don't think so. After all, it's a time when we are enjoying the exhilaration of victory, the spoils of the battle, or a time when there is much excitement. How can we possibly be vulnerable at such a time?" On the other hand, it is a time when there is renewed self-confidence, when we feel we can conquer any foe, and can be victorious over any obstacle that might confront us. Do you see that our focus has suddenly changed and that we have quickly forgotten where we received our strength? You might say, "But that is just a little thing; surely such thoughts cannot be harmful to us."

Let me ask you: Where would we be if God lifted His hand of mercy from us but for a moment? Where would we be were it not for His grace? David realized this when he wrote in Psalm 124: 2, 3,

"If the Lord had not been on our side when men attacked us, when their anger flared against us, they would have swallowed us alive." Solomon said in Lamentations 3:22, 23, "Because of the Lord's great love, we are not consumed, for his compassions never fail. They are new every morning; great is your faithfulness."

I thought, what a graphic picture of the "little sins" in our lives. Solomon said, "The little foxes ruin the vineyard." When the vineyard is sweetened with the scented blossoms and the tiny grapes begin to appear, they need to be guarded and protected, lest the little foxes come in and destroy them. We often think of big sins that are so detrimental to us. But God sees it differently; He looks upon the heart. He sees the anger, the resentment, an unforgiving spirit, bitterness, selfishness, pride, and many other "sins within." The result is that, He lifts His Hand of blessing from us, our testimony loses its effectiveness, the joy of the Lord fades into the past, and we become defeated, discouraged, and useless spiritually. The "little foxes" have ruined the spiritual vineyard of our life.

Our most vulnerable time is right after our greatest victory. Why? Because we feel confident, self-assured, and secure, and we take things into our own hands and proceed without God. We simply say, not out loud, but certainly within our hearts, "I don't need God for this. I can handle it; this is a piece of cake." What happens? We presume upon the goodness of God. We expect His help, but we neglect to call upon Him in prayer. There is no dependence upon God, no searching of our hearts, no preparation for the enemy, no cleansing, no faith in God. We just plunge ahead in the weakness of our own ability, and we crash-land. Solomon said, "Trust in the Lord with all your heart, and lean not unto your own understanding. In all your ways acknowledge Him, and He will direct your path." We must ever keep our eyes fixed upon the Lord. It is He who gives us the victory and guards us against the "little foxes" that would destroy us. Oh that we might trust Him completely!

Live as Children of the Light

"For you were once darkness, but now you are light in the Lord. Live as children of light (for the fruit of the Spirit consist in all goodness, righteousness and truth) and find out what pleases the Lord." Ephesians 5:8-10

What do you think it means to "live as children of the light"? We may get some idea of our duty and its meaning when we search the heavens. The stars are all illuminated by the sun. They have no capacity within themselves to shine so brightly but simply "reflect the light" of the sun. They impart to us the light they have received from the Sun. So we are reflectors of the Son of Righteousness, imparting the light we receive from Him. Within ourselves we have no capacity to reflect the "brightness of His glory." Paul says we must "shine forth as lights in the world, holding forth the Word of Life, making our light to so shine before men that they see our good works and glorify our Father which is in heaven."

Paul's appeal is made from what we were, once darkness, to what we are, light in the Lord. We are to live in keeping with what we are "in Christ." The fruit of such a life is expressed in our life as "goodness, righteousness, and truth." It is His Life being lived through us, proving what is acceptable unto the Lord. To live as children of the light, we will delight to do His will, walk in the way of His Commandments, hearkening unto the voice of His Word, and making every step a prelude to our "walking worthy of the Lord unto all."

HOW are we to live? Paul says in Ephesians 5:15-21, "Be very careful, therefore, how you live, not as unwise but as wise, making the most of every opportunity, because the days are evil. Therefore do not be foolish, but understand what the Lord's will is. Do not get drunk with wine, which leads to debauchery. Instead, be filled with the Spirit. Speak to one another with psalms, hymns, and spiritual songs. Sing and make music in your heart to the Lord, always giving thanks to God the Father for everything, in the name of our Lord Jesus Christ. Submit to one another out of reverence for Christ."

To so "LIVE" is the work of the Holy Spirit in our lives. The Greek word for "be" in this verse is in a tense that emphasizes "continual action," meaning to "be constantly filled." We will not receive "more of His Spirit" than when we were initially saved. But so often, the Holy Spirit does not have full and free access to all of our lives. He therefore is quenched, saddened, and grieved. God's desire is that every Believer be "continually filled to overflowing," a daily yielding to the Spirit so that He may fill our lives afresh to an "overflowing measure."

It is our privilege to be "filled with the Spirit" according to our capacity, having all of our faculties and powers subject to His control. BY HIM, our understanding may be enlightened, so that we will "view everything from a Godly perspective." BY HIM, our will may be regulated to be "conformed to the Mind and Will of God." BY HIM, our affections will be set aflame so that the "whole of our personality will be melted and cast into the very mold of Christ." Being "filled with the Spirit" IS NOT receiving more of the Spirit; rather, it is the SPIRIT POSSESSING MORE OF US!

Be an Encourager

"I tell you the truth, whatever you did for the least of these brothers of mine, you did for me." Matthew 25:40

When I was a boy, our scoutmaster told us about the characteristics of a rope. Rope is made strong by the fabric that's used, even stronger by the number of corded, interwoven strands. What a beautiful picture of the corded strands of support God provides for our Spiritual Journey. He has provided His Word, the Holy Spirit, His promises, His faithfulness, the magnitude of His Majesty, the fellowship of Believers, access into His presence by prayer, and many more. When woven together, they give us His Divine Strength.

One of the corded strands we often neglect is being AN ENCOURAGER to others. People all around us are hurting, fearful, without friends, and many are without hope. They do not know how to pray or trust the Lord in their discouraging dilemmas. You say, "Well, how does that affect me?" One of the great needs among Christians is to be sensitive to the needs of others, to have an open heart ready to respond to those in difficult situations. We need to encourage others with a heart of love and let them know we care. God said, "I sought for a man among them that should make up the hedge, and stand in the gap before me, but I found none." We need to make ourselves available to stand in the gap, to have an ear to listen to heartaches, to have a spirit to respond and communicate to others, so they will know we are ready to reach out to them in sincere Godly love. To be used by the Lord in this way could turn their lives around with new hope, determination, and perseverance. How should we respond to people that are not pleasant to us, or not of our choosing? Do we respond to the prompting of His Love that seeks to care and comfort, to strengthen and encourage them in their need? Are we willing to give unto others the hand of assurance, or a heart of love, which will lift their life from despair to hope, from discouragement to renewed strength, from loneliness to the joy of knowing that God loves them and cares for them?

Michael Green, in his book *"1500 Illustrations for Biblical Preaching,"* tells a striking story of Benjamin West. When West was a young boy, he decided to paint a picture of his sister while his mother was away from home. He lined up his assorted colors of paint and started. Soon he had an awful mess of paint that had made its way everywhere but on the picture. His mother eventually returned and saw the awful mess he had created. Instead of scolding him, she picked up the portrait and said, "What a beautiful portrait of your sister!" Then she kissed him. Later in life, when he had gained success and international fame as an artist, he spoke before a large, distinguished audience that had gathered to honor him. At the close of his address, he reflected upon this experience and said, "With that kiss and word of encouragement, I became an artist." It was the encouragement of wisdom and an act of love that was the turning point that gave motivation, perseverance, and determination to maximize his gift and ability. Let us buy up every opportunity as an occasion to manifest His Love and to encourage someone in desperate need! You may be the only one sent to encourage him!

Hearken and Do ... Live and Possess

"Hear now, O Israel, the decrees and laws I am about to teach you. Follow them so that you may live and may go in and take possession of the land that the Lord, the God of your fathers, is giving you." Deuteronomy 4:1

*M*oses proclaims the universal, abiding principal that is evident throughout the Scriptures: Hearken unto the Word of God: make His commandments the rule of your life, so you shall live abundantly in His companionship, and you will possess all that He wants to do in and through your life. The true pathway of life and the secret of possessing your possessions is simple obedience to the Commandments of God.

God has given us His Word, not to speculate upon or critically debate its issues, but to be instructed by it and to walk in obedience to it. John makes this very clear. "If anyone loves me, he will obey my teaching. My Father will love him, and we will come to him and make our home with him." What a tremendous promise! He has not only promised to love us but to manifest Himself to us. It would be a serious mistake to think that every Believer enjoyed the blessing of this promise; they do not! This promise is only to those who yield in loving obedience to His commandments. It lies within the reach of all, but all do not enjoy it, because they are not walking in obedience to His Word or delighting themselves in Him

We see this graphically illustrated in our families. There are two sons. One thinks only of himself, doing his will, and gratifying his own desires. He does not seek to be with his father and takes no pleasure in his father's interests. He has no desire to carry out his father's wishes or seek to know his mind. He avails himself of all the benefits of a son, but never seeks to gratify the father's heart with loving attention to his will.

The other son is the direct opposite. He delights in being with his father, loves his interests, his ways, and his words. He seeks to carry out his father's wishes, seeks to be agreeable and supportive. He loves his father, not for the inheritance, but for himself and the joy of doing his will. He seeks to gratify his father in loving obedience and is grateful to be his son. There is great joy in satisfying the heart of his father.

We have no difficulty seeing how differently the father feels toward these sons. He can have no pleasure in the willful, self-indulgent, careless son. He will occupy much of his thoughts with anxious concerns for his welfare and will spend sleepless nights thinking and praying for him. He will spend and be spent for him. But he does not agree with him or condone his lifestyle. He does not possess his confidence or freely seek to influence his choices. He cannot be in close fellowship with his thoughts and actions.

How graphically this plays out in the lives of Christians today. God manifests Himself to His obedient children, to those who keep His commandments and do them, who delight in His Word and seek to do His will. What the Lord has done for us through His love and grace should occupy the first place in our hearts. There should be a heavy responsibility within our hearts to walk circumspectly before others in submission and humility before God. We should respond with "implicit obedience."

Hear, O Lord...Guard My Life...Have Mercy on Me

"Hear, O Lord, and answer me: for I am poor and needy. Guard my life, for I am devoted to you. You are my God; save your servant who trusts in you. Have mercy on me, O Lord, for I call to you all day long." Psalm 86:1-3

The effectiveness of our prayers depends largely on our perspective of the Majesty of God, our concept of WHO GOD IS, and our understanding in knowing who we are before Him. Acknowledging our utter dependence upon Him, our faith in His unchanging character, and our confidence in knowing He loves and cares for us will give Him free access to manifest His plan and purpose in our lives.

As we grow in grace and in an abiding companionship with Him, we will experience the excellence of a life in communion with Him, where our thoughts and actions are in the "attitude of prayer," and our walk with Him becomes a life of sacrifice and praise, adoration and worship. We shall know what David experienced, abiding "under the shadow of the Almighty," walking in the consciousness of His Presence, and experiencing the path of life with Him as our Divine Guide. Charles Spurgeon said, "God is too good to be unkind, too wise to be mistaken. When you cannot trace His Hand, you can always trust His Heart."

"In the day of trouble, I will call upon thee, for thou wilt answer me. Teach me thy way, O Lord." Isn't it interesting to observe that David desired to be "taught" in the way of God? He recognized his own inability and his own limitations in knowing God's way, and he sought for God to reveal "the way" unto him. This required of him a receptive spirit and a responsive heart. The servant of God will be sustained, preserved, kept, and upheld in life's circumstances as he earnestly prays and abides in Him. The servant's "path and service" must come from the servant's Lord. His way and will can be ascertained only by His Word and through prayer. God said, "I will teach thee in the way thou shall go, I will guide thee with mine eye."

David cried out to God in the midst of his troubles, "Teach me thy way, O Lord! I will walk in thy truth. Unite my heart to fear thee." Frustrated, confused, weary, pursued by Saul, David was stirred up to a greater desire after God. He was determined to seek God with all of his heart. He wanted his spirit to be united in oneness with Him. So often we are guilty of countless diversions that distract, spoil, dilute, and affect our positive pursuit in our walk with God. May the Lord deliver us from entanglements with meaningless endeavours. We must pursue with singleness of heart and purpose if we are to be led in His way and His will.

There are two requisites for an acceptable walk with the Lord. First, we may know His way by an illumination of our mind. Secondly, our walk must be focused on Christ. He will not honor or guide a "divided heart." There is a "singleness of heart" (Acts 2:46) that is indispensable to walking rightly with God and being led by Him. Oh that we might cry unto the Lord, that we may be taught the way of His will and purpose for us! Our responsibility is to walk in obedience; the results are His responsibility. Dare to trust and obey!

They Have Left Off to Take Heed

"For they shall eat, and not have enough: they shall commit whoredom, and shall not increase: because they have left off to take heed to the Lord." Hosea 4:10

The eternal measure of our life must be the standard of His Word, no other. God's Word makes it very clear how we should live, the attitude that should govern our disposition, and the focus that will determine the path that we follow. Satan has many ways to divert the attention of our hearts from being steadfastly fixed on God.

Unless we find God in our quiet times, in reading His Word, in relating every part of our lives to His Principles and Truth, in desiring and seeking His will, walking in His way, opening up our hearts to the work of the Holy Spirit, and responding with a willing spirit, our lives will become recipients of Satan's insidious ways. If we omit any of these spiritual virtues from our daily life, it isn't long until our life begins to manifest the very things that are contrary to the will of God. We unknowingly become vulnerable and responsive to attitudes and actions against the very truth and life we once held as the Standard of Truth by which we lived. You say, "Oh, that won't happen to me." The Scriptures say, "Wherefore let him that thinks he stands take heed lest he fall." We undermine our lives with self-confidence and independence, we lean on fleshly resources rather than recognize our inability to stand against the resources of Satan, and we fail to lean upon the eternal strength of God.

It happens constantly among Believers, Christian workers, and pastors. It all begins when we take our eyes off of the "fixed position of our faith," Jesus Christ. Often times, our focus is diverted to secondary carnal pursuits that not only damage our testimony but also destroy our spiritual lives. We fill our lives with things, which may be good in themselves in many cases, but which become destructive when they crowd out other things. We need to spend time and energy on things that will encourage our growth in grace, build up our faith, and cause our lives to be an encouragement, a strength, a challenge, and a blessing to others.

Let me ask you to consider prayerfully these questions:

If we knew in a measure God's Power and Majesty, would we dare to provoke Him by our evil thoughts and sinful ways?

If we could behold God's Holiness, would we consider sin so passively and give no thought to the gross evil of our actions?

If we could appraise God's Justice, would we think that God in the Day of Judgment would simply overlook our sins and iniquities?

If we knew God's Mercy to us in Christ Jesus, would we give so little thought and consideration to His infinite provision for us?

If we knew God's Matchless Grace, would we gloat in our pride and arrogance, concerned only with our own interests and our self-centered lives?

To KNOW HIM is to spend time with Him, letting Him reveal His love afresh and anew unto us, and to spend time reading the Word to know His will and way. Oh that we might cry out with David, "Search me, O God, and know my heart: try me, and know my thoughts: And see if there be any wicked way in me, and lead me in the way everlasting."

Hear the Word of the Lord

"Hear the word of the Lord, you Israelites, because the Lord has a charge to bring against you who live in the land: There is no faithfulness, no love, no acknowledgment of God in the land." Hosea 4:1

*I*magine a dusty old prophet coming into a city in Israel, taking his stand at the gate or next to a place of worship where many are gathered, and daring to point his finger at them and proclaim these condemning words from God: "The Lord has a charge to bring against you who live in the land." There was great prosperity. They were living off the fat of the land, and here was an old prophet talking about the "judgment of God." WHY? "Because there was no faithfulness, no love, no acknowledgment of God. Because of this, the land mourns and all who live in it waste away."

First, they had abandoned the principles of certainty, dependability, truth and reliability, which mark them out as a "people of God." When He called them out of Egypt, He said unto them, "You are to walk in my commandments and according to my statutes." Your life is going to be a demonstration of my holiness and my truthfulness. You haven't lived that way. There is no faithfulness or evidence of your loyalty to God.

Secondly, there is no kindness or sense of God's lovingkindness. You have the Covenant, the Law, the Commandments, the things I have instructed you to do, but you are not applying these to your life. They are but symbols of God's Truth.

Thirdly, there is no acknowledgment of God. He is not saying they do not know about God, but that they have forgotten WHO HE IS, do not acknowledge God as Sovereign, or do not recognize His right to reign as the Lord of their lives. The reality of God was not a practical part of their everyday life. Their concept of God was, "He's out there somewhere, some place, but I do not relate to Him."

What are you doing to acknowledge God in your life? You might say, "I'm teaching a Sunday School class, serving as a deacon, on the church board, singing in the choir, or any number of things within the church. This I do." More important, HOW do you acknowledge God in your ministry? Is there evidence of His Love being manifested through your life? Is there a compassionate heart for those to whom you minister? Is there a servant's attitude of intentional commitment before God? Is your heart humble and contrite before God? Do you seek the empowering of the Holy Spirit for your ministry? Are there manifestations of Covenant loyalty, faithfulness, and loving-kindness? Do others see Christ magnified in your life and ministry? There's a difference between being a "religious activist" and being serious about your spiritual relationship with God, following Him as His servant and disciple.

Our concern, like Hosea's concern regarding Israel in his day, should be, "How can I make the Truths and Principles of God's Word applicable to all of my daily routines and envelope the whole of my life? So that what I do, where I go, what I say, what I think, and my attitudes will demonstrate that I am a servant of Christ! The reality of Christ living within our lives makes a clear distinction between "being religious" and "being spiritual" as God would have us be. Search your heart "at the foot of the cross."

He Washed and Came Seeing

"And he said unto him, Go, wash in the pool of Siloam (which is by interpretation, Sent). He went his way, therefore, and washed, and came seeing." John 9:7

Two things taking place in this incident in which Jesus heals the man who was blind from birth, are always evident when God works in or through us. They are very closely linked to our spiritual journey and are essential to an effective and fruitful walk with the Lord. They are OBEDIENCE and FAITH. The blind man obeyed what Jesus instructed him to do, and he went forth to the pool of Siloam and washed his eyes in faith. The result was that he received his sight. God always manifests His Presence and Power in the lives of Believers who walk in obedience, exercise faith, and give God His rightful place as Sovereign in their lives.

The Pharisees were outraged at this miracle, and proclaimed Christ as a sinner for having "worked" on the Sabbath. In their opinion, spitting on the ground to make clay to anoint the blind man's eyes was breaking the law. They were more interested in the "letter of the law" than in the miracle that had taken place when the blind man received his sight. But those who had known the blind man were astounded and sought an explanation. They took him to the Pharisees, who questioned him and his parents. Finally, the blind man simply said with conviction and authority, "One thing I know, that whereas I was blind, NOW I SEE."

The Pharisees could not deny the miracle that stood so convincingly before them. When I read this incident, I thought, "Wouldn't it be wonderful if our lives were so transformed by the power of God that we would also be a miracle of God's mighty power?" The love of God would be so evident in our lives that people would wonder what had taken place! That happened to Peter and John when they were brought before the Sadducees and were questioned about the impotent man being healed. When they examined Peter and John and "perceived they were unlearned and ignorant men, they marvelled." The only explanation they could give was, "They had been with Jesus." "Beholding the man, they could say nothing."

Shouldn't we live our lives so that our attitudes, conversation, and walk will be evidence of His Life being lived through us? Shouldn't the fruit of the Spirit be seen in our lives "by purity, by knowledge, by long-suffering, by kindness, by the Holy Ghost, by love unfeigned," so that there will be no doubt that we have been with Jesus? Such has been the testimony of many who have turned their lives over to the Lordship of Christ. They have come to a freedom and release from the bondage of a self-centered life. When Christ is given the authority of our lives, when we surrender unto Him our will to control our lives, then He gives unto us HIS LIFE, that will reflect the "fruit of the Spirit" unto others. Then our lives, like that of the blind man who received his sight, will be miracles of His grace and will magnify the One who did it all, JESUS OUR LORD! Wouldn't you like this to be true in your life? It can WHEN YOU WALK IN OBEDIENCE AND DARE TO BELIEVE!

Ruth Clave Unto Her

"And they lifted up their voice and wept again: and Orpah kissed her mother-in-law; but Ruth clave unto her." Ruth 1:14

Tragedy struck the family of Naomi after it left Bethlehem to seek out an existence in Moab. Elimelech, her husband, and Mahlon and Chilion, her sons, all died in Moab, leaving her a widow with two daughters-in-law, in a foreign country. She suggests that her daughters-in-law return to their homes, and she will go back to her friends in Bethlehem. The scene that follows is both "tragic" and "blessed." It's very instructive to notice what these two young women chose to do. Their decision would affect the rest of their lives.

It was a sad time for all of them as they wept, realizing their tragic past and the prospects of a bleak future. Now notice, Orpah loved Naomi, her mother-in-law, but the love that never fails was not there. At first, she was inclined to go, but when the facts were laid out before her, pointing out the sacrifices she would have to make, she returned to her own people and to her idolatrous gods. Orpah lost everything she was seeking and missed all that God would have done for her. Orpah made a tragic decision to forsake the "God of Israel" and was the recipient of its sad consequences.

Ruth's decision was quite different. She declared her love and affection to Naomi in such beautiful and meaningful words, from the depth of a heart of love. Listen to these heart-moving words of Ruth: "Entreat me not to leave you, or to return from following after you: for wherever you go, I will go; and wherever you lodge, I will lodge: your people shall be my people, and your God my God: where you die, will I die, and there will I be buried: the Lord do so to me, and more also, if aught but death part thee and me."

The tremendous message that has been a challenge to me since I first read the book of Ruth is this: All that Ruth was to become was the result of what she "saw and learned of God in the life of Naomi," her mother-in-law. Now think that through. What an impact Naomi's life had on Ruth! Ruth's life was changed forever!

Through all the heartache, sorrow, and suffering Naomi went through with her family, Ruth observed closely and saw a depth of commitment in her mother-in-law that shone forth in her darkest hours. She saw in Naomi an "unwavering faith in God" that overcame the most difficult circumstances. She saw an "uncompromising spirit" that stood true, regardless of how devastating life had been to Naomi. She saw a "dedication to God" that led Naomi to instruct Ruth of her faith in the God of Israel. When the time came for their separation, there was no way Ruth was going to leave Naomi. She was more precious to her than anything she had known before. She broke away from everything that was not of God, to take refuge under the shadow of His Wings, the God of Israel! What an eternal impact Naomi's life had on Ruth!

What impact does your life have on those closest to you, to others that your life touches every day? Does your life reflect the commitment, devotion, and love that Ruth saw in Naomi? What do others see when they observe your life? Do they see Jesus? THIS IS GOD'S CHALLENGE UNTO YOU TODAY!

He Which Hath Begun...
Will Perform It

"Being confident of this very thing, that he which hath begun a good work in you will perform it until the day of Jesus Christ." Philippians 1:6

*P*aul and Timothy rejoiced in being bondservants together with the Believers at Philippi, as partners together in the fellowship of the Gospel. They shared in the trials, labors, and conflicts they encountered. It was difficult for the Believers to take a stand for Christ, to declare their faith amidst idolatrous people, while trying to be built up in the their faith. Paul assures them of his prayers. Thankful for every remembrance of them, he encourages them, "Being confident of this very thing, that he which hath begun a good work in you, will perform it [will bring it to maturity, will complete His plan and purpose in your life] until the day of Jesus Christ."

Paul prays for four specific things that he desires for them. That your love may abound more and more in knowledge and in all judgment, that ye may approve things that are excellent, that ye may be sincere and without offense, and that ye be filled with the fruits of righteousness. [We also need to be included in this prayer.] Before these Believers could live exemplary lives, the "overflowing love of Christ" needed to envelope their lives by the Holy Spirit, so that they would be able to perceive, understand and discern not only what is right, but what is best and foremost. Norman Grubb, the son-in-law of C. T. Studd, the founder of the Heart of Africa Mission, said, "It's wonderful to be filled with the Holy Spirit, but God wants to fill our cups to overflowing. Only when our cups overflow with His Spirit can He maximize our lives to be effective and fruitful." May the Holy Spirit spill out of our cups in an abundant measure to others!

Paul wanted their lives to be pure and blameless so that they would be filled with the fruits of righteousness. The Greek word for "pure" has two possible meanings. First, "to be judged by sunlight" and to stand the test of close examination. Second, "to shake as a sieve," so that after the shaking, only the pure substance remains. In the refining of gold, the refiner sits by his crucible and heats the gold, removing all the impurities as they rise to the surface from the intense heat. He continues until he can "see the reflection of his face" in the melted gold. God does not sift and refine us in relaxed and comfortable circumstances, but rather in times of anxiety and adversity, in days of stress and trial. Paul says to put your confidence in HIS FAITHFULNESS!

In her devotional classic "*Streams in the Desert,*" Mrs. Charles Cowan wrote, "Sometimes God sends severe blasts of trial upon His children to develop their graces. Just as torches burn most brightly when swung to and fro, just as the juniper smells sweetest when flung into the flames, so the rich qualities of a Christian often come out under the North Wind of suffering and adversity. Bruised hearts often emit the fragrance of a sweet savour that God loves to smell." What He begins, He will bring to completion!

May we continually search our hearts to remove all sin and impurities that might cause others to stumble, "that we might walk worthy of the Lord, pleasing unto all, being fruitful in every good work, and increasing in the knowledge of God." Is this the desire of your heart? Let Christ reign as Lord and Sovereign!

Ye Thought Evil Against Me, but God Meant It Unto Good

"But as for you, ye thought evil against me; but God meant it unto good, to bring to pass, as it is this day, to save much people alive." Genesis 50:20

*O*ne of the most touching accounts in all of the Scriptures is the story of Joseph, who was a type of Christ in so many ways. I never read these verses without being deeply moved in my heart and spirit. When he stood before his brothers, who had so maliciously betrayed him and sold him to strangers because of their jealousy and envy, Joseph caused all of his attendants to leave, "and he wept aloud; and the Egyptians and the house of Pharaoh heard." With a heart that was torn by love, he said unto his brothers, "I am Joseph!" Can you imagine such a scene! LOVE embraces jealousy, hate, envy, pride, and betrayal, and CONQUERS THEM! Joseph said to his brothers, "Ye thought evil against me, but God meant it unto good."

What do you think was going through the minds of his brothers? Certainly they deserved his scorn and revenge, to be thrown into prison, or to be punished for the hatred and persecution they inflicted upon Joseph. Joseph could have related his years of suffering, the false accusation of a crime he utterly abhorred, and his stay in prison, where for a time he was "laid in iron" and constrained by heavy fetters. (Psalm 105:18) When he entreated the Pharaoh's butler to intercede for him, he forgot him. Years of waiting, wondering "how these things could possibly be," knowing the bent of his heart for God, yet bound in an Egyptian prison with no hope of getting out.

BUT GOD, in His providence, had His hand on Joseph through it all! Let me bring to your attention a principle that we should never forget. God's purposes for Joseph were accomplished by the very means used to defeat them. At every turn, Satan sought to discourage and defeat Joseph, to assault and destroy the "plan of God" for His devoted servant, Joseph, but to no avail. In "God's time and God's way," He exalted Joseph to be second only to Pharaoh, to be the supreme governor of the Egyptian kingdom, and all were ordered to bow their knees to Joseph. (Genesis 41:43) God exalted him to be both "the shepherd and the stone of Israel," that he might not only provide for Egypt and the neighboring kingdoms, but also be an effectual support to all his kindred, and preserve the lives of those very persons who had sought his destruction.

We cannot understand many of the things that take place in our lives. We are absolutely bewildered and, like Joseph, wonder how it can be happening. But God has His time, His means, and His way. If we follow in faith, "daring to believe" in His faithfulness and loving care, we will see His Hand in it all when He brings us through our "wilderness" to His appointed place. His way to glory was through the anguish and agony of Gethsemane. His way to the Crown was by the way of the cross. So, in our lives, there must be the "molding, melting, making process" that He takes us through, that we might "be conformed to the image of his Son." Is this not your desire? Then we, like Joseph, must keep our eyes fixed on Him, "looking unto Jesus, the author and finisher of our faith." Let us then wait for HIS TIME, HIS WAY, HIS WILL!

The Lord Is My Shepherd

"The Lord is my shepherd; I shall not be in want." Psalm 23:1

*T*his is probably the most familiar portion of the Scriptures, recognized by all mankind, yet one of the least understood and appropriately applied to our lives. Many know in mind and thought what is written in most of the Scriptures, but have never applied its truth to their hearts and lives. Even among Believers, few lay hold of the tremendous truth within these few words. They are monumental. Making them a reality in our lives will be transforming. Let's look at this first verse and try to understand its great truth and the enormity of its application to our lives.

"The Lord is my Shepherd." First of all, this Shepherd is different than any other. He is THE Shepherd, sent by God, anointed of God. He is THE Shepherd for specific sheep. He is the Shepherd WHO IS THE LORD OF ALL, God manifested in the flesh, the Creator of all things. He is the Shepherd who ministers and cares for my present and future needs. Then David very meaningfully says, "He is MY Shepherd." What a difference a personal relationship makes in any acquaintance. This is what makes Christianity different and unique from all other religions. We can have a personal relationship with God through Jesus Christ our Saviour and our Shepherd. This gives unto all who trust Him great promise and enormous meaning in their lives. He becomes intimately involved in all things.

And what does this personal relationship mean? "I shall not want." Wow! What else needs to be said? What an all-inclusive statement! I shall not want what? Whatever need God allows is for my good and His glory! This includes all of my life – past, present, and future; my well-being and existence; my relationship to everyone, everywhere! You might say, "What then is my problem, if I have such a Great Shepherd?" The problem is not with the Shepherd; it rests with us, whether intentional or not. Our concept of the Great Shepherd is limited to the boundaries of our own making. We view Him in impersonal generalities and confine Him to the limitations of our own understanding. We bring Him down to our finite human reasoning, thereby taking away His supernatural attributes.

When He is truly MY Shepherd, how can there be any need? He has promised "to supply all of our need according to his riches in glory by Christ Jesus." David says, "I shall not want." He is my ALL SUFFICIENT SHEPHERD. I am in His perfect care, protection, concern, and provision. I can be utterly content, not craving or seeking for anything more. Jesus said, "I am the good shepherd: the good shepherd gives his life for his sheep." The remainder of this wonderful Psalm rests on this verse and explains why He is the Good and All Sufficient Shepherd and why "I shall not want."

Oh to find Him as the "Shepherd of our life" in our everyday walk and to see Him lead us into all the ventures of the remaining verses! We can say with David, "The Lord Is My Shepherd; I Shall Not Want."

He Makes Me to Lie Down

"He makes me to lie down in green pastures. He leads me beside the quiet waters." Psalm 23:2

This verse speaks of a contentment that we seldom find in a world with its gear in "fast forward." I have often wondered why we are "programmed" to live at such a torrid pace, always on the go, surrounded by all kinds of things that compete for our time, energy, and interests. We do not seem to know what to do with ourselves, for some strange reason, when we are in an atmosphere of quiet bliss. We are like a roaring race car that just pulled into "pit road" with our engine racing. We are impatient and raring to go, but we have to stop to refuel. We can't wait to get on the track again and continue the race. Why do we yield to the frustrating confusion and illusive attractions of our environment that seek to control our lives? I'm afraid many of us yield to the pressure and course of the world. Such a lifestyle diverts the focus of our lives, robs us of precious time, and destroys what we need to do so desperately, to BE STILL AND KNOW THAT I AM GOD!

David had pressure from all sides with continual agitation from his enemies, turmoil from the people he served as king, and conflict from the adversary of his soul. How blessed it must had been when he came apart and enjoyed the quiet retreat and inspirational green pastures to simply lie down in peaceful reflection. How needful this is in our lives today. It is in the solemn stillness of God's Presence that we can hear His still, small voice saying unto us, "Peace, be still." It is there that we can be blessedly consumed with ALL HE IS and ALL HE WANTS TO BE TO US.

Phillip Keller, in his book *"A Shepherd Looks at Psalm 23,"* tells how sheep refuse to lie down unless they are free from all fear. When alarmed by an unknown noise or a suspected prey, they panic, without knowing what the danger is. Nothing quiets or reassures the sheep like the appearance of the shepherd in the field. Our Good Shepherd dispels our fear, panic, and terror of the unknown in our lives. "For God hath not given to us the spirit of fear, but of power, and love, and of a sound mind."

The companion of lying down in "green pastures" is being led beside the "still waters." Can you imagine how refreshing it must have been for the hot and weary sheep to be led by the shepherd to the still, clear water of a mountain stream to be restored by its cool water and receive newness of life? We seek everywhere to quench our thirst for God with programs, activities, spiritual involvement, and a host of other things, which will never satisfy our quest for God. How blessed it is to find God's provision for our thirst as He "leads me beside the still waters" to the Fountainhead, JESUS.

Jesus said, "If any man is thirsty, let him come unto me and drink. He who believes in me, as the Scripture hath said, from his innermost being shall flow rivers of living water." Oh to be refreshed, restored, and revived by the Fountain of Living Water, Jesus Christ. I trust today that He will make you to "lie down in green pastures" and be led "beside the still waters" IN HIS PRESENCE!

He Restores My Soul

"He restores my soul." Psalm 23:3

*S*urely, anyone in the care of the Good Shepherd has experienced the need for restoration. To think differently is to deny the reality of life with its many devastating circumstances. God did not promise we would not have difficulties, but He did promise He would be our sufficiency in them. David knew what it was to be "cast down," to be in constant danger and fear, without resources and strength. He cried out, "Why art thou cast down, O my soul? Why art thou disquieted within me? Hope thou in God." What does it mean to be cast down?

Paul knew what it meant to be cast down, to be in desperate need, to have no resources within yourself to rise above your need, or to withstand the difficulty you encounter. He said, "We are troubled on every side, yet not distressed; we are perplexed, but not in despair; persecuted, but not forsaken; 'cast down', but not destroyed." Paul knew the comfort and care of the Good Shepherd. Sometimes a sheep finds himself on his back, unable to right himself. He becomes frightful and he panics. Unless the Shepherd finds him and sets him aright, he will perish from his pathetic dilemma. How blessed to know that God, Our Good Shepherd, comes and ministers unto us as the shepherd of the sheep does. Upon finding a cast-down sheep, the shepherd must restore it with loving comfort and tender care. He restores peace where fear and panic abound while physically ministering to the needs that have resulted from this dreadful experience. Slowly but surely, the shepherd restores the sheep and takes him back to the fold.

What a beautiful picture of compassion, concern, and care of Our Good Shepherd. Like the sheep, we are frustrated, fearful, and often panicky in our devastating circumstances. We search for help but find none, until we turn our hearts in faith to our Good Shepherd who is ever sensitive to our needs. Our Shepherd is always ready to rescue and restore, to comfort and care, and knows just what we need. He comes to where we are, helpless, needy, and fearful, and restores us as He "leads us in the paths of righteousness for His Name's sake."

This is the heart of Christ, our Good Shepherd. Many erroneously think that God becomes disgusted, fed up, and furious with Believers who fall or become frustrated, helpless, and spiritually vexed. Let me ask you, "How did Christ deal with Peter when he denied the Lord in the palace courtyard?" As they took him out, Christ looked at Peter, not with scorn and hate, but with eyes of compassion, love, and divine patience. He dealt with Peter so he might be tenderly restored.

Can we not look back over our lives and remember times when we had fallen, were overcome with fear, had no one to turn to, and were desperate and without hope, until our blessed Lord put his loving arms around us and restored us? How blessed to know the Shepherd Who found us, for "He restores my soul." Jesus our Shepherd, who ever seeks to bring us back into the blessed relationship with the Father, has promised, "I will never leave you or forsake you." Bless the Lord!

He Guides Me in Paths of Righteousness

"He guides me in paths of righteousness for his name's sake.
Psalm 23:3

*H*ave you ever stopped to consider what it really means to be led in the "paths of righteousness for His name's sake"? First of all, what does God mean by the paths of righteousness? Did you notice that we are led in these paths "for His Name's sake"? Interesting, isn't it? You might say, "I always thought He led me in these paths for my sake." That's part of it, but we must remember that we bear His virtues, reflect His truth, and seek to uphold His Holy Name. Our considerations are secondary. First and foremost, HE IS TO BE MAGNIFIED in our lives. Therefore, He primarily leads us in the "paths of righteousness for His Name's sake." Look what God said to Israel through Ezekiel: "It is not for your sake, O house of Israel, but for the sake of my holy name. I will give you a new heart and put a new spirit in you. I will remove your heart of stone and give you a heart of flesh." It is "His glory" that's at stake, "His honor" that's involved, and "His integrity" that's in view in the preservation of His sheep. Therefore, He never withdraws His lovingkindness from us, nor ceases to watch over and care for us. God cherishes the well being of His own, and seeks to so lead us, that we will be conformed to the image of His Son and reflect His glory.

What are these "paths of righteousness"? Notice that they are "paths," not just a path. If we would think through the many encounters in our life where He has led us, we will find that many paths have been involved as He has led us. We cannot look at a current situation and say, "Well, the Lord led me in this way before, and He will do the same this time." Not necessarily. He chooses the path most suitable for our good, and for His glory. Could we ask for any better path to be led in or a better Shepherd to lead us?

Phillip Keller, in his book *"A Shepherd Looks at Psalm 23,"* describes sheep. "Sheep, like us, are notorious creatures of habit. They follow the same trails until they become ruts, graze in the same fields until they are barren, and pollute the same ground until it is corrupt. They are dumb, stubborn, prefer to do what they have always done, and go their own way, regardless of what the consequences may incur. That's why it is so important for the shepherd to lead them in the right paths, to the right pastures, to the quiet pastures, beside the still waters. Their welfare is his priority and his utmost concern. The sheep reflect the integrity, leadership, and care of the shepherd."

We, too, are stubborn, self-willed, proud, self-sufficient, and determined that we know best. Therefore, we go our own way. Isaiah said, "All we like sheep have gone astray; we have turned everyone to his own way." Solomon said, "There is a way that seems right unto a man, but the end thereof are the ways of death." And Jesus said, "I am the way, the truth, and the life." This is our pivotal point. We either follow the Shepherd in a path that is right, or we continue along our ill-trodden way of fruitlessness, despair, frustration, and failure. HOW BLESSED IT IS TO FOLLOW THE GOOD SHEPHERD, FOR HIS NAME'S SAKE!

I Will Fear No Evil for Thou Art With Me

"Even though I walk through the valley of the shadow of death, I will fear no evil; for you are with me." Psalm 23:4

All of us are given experiences in life, when we are called to walk through the agonizing valley of the shadow of death. The "valleys" touch us in every stratum of mankind, and their effects and results vary to a great extent. Going through these valleys is a heart-wrenching and soul-searching experience. Some become bitter and resentful, some distraught and lonely, others are perplexed and frustrated, and still others simply lose it altogether. They cannot cope with the devastating demands, and they become emotionally despondent.

God has given precious promises in His Word to assure Christians of His presence with them, His Care and Comfort for them, and His Sufficiency to enable and strengthen them through their dark hours of need. It is in these dreadful experiences that Jesus says unto us, "I will never leave thee nor forsake thee." We all will have valleys, disappointments, afflictions, trials, discouragement, despair, loneliness, and other dark and difficult days. But these need not be disasters. They can be the most blessed and productive times in our lives. Often, God uses these "valley times" as turning points in our lives and awakens us to a new awareness of the greatness of God. When our attitude is one of quiet acceptance of His leading, confident trust in His faithfulness, and assured hope "that all things work together for good to those who are called according to His purpose," we can rest triumphantly! How comforting to know He will walk with us through the valley.

It is in our "valley experience" that our faith is stretched, but made steadfast. Our walk is weak, but we are made stronger. Our way is dreary and dark, but He is the Light of our life. Our hope is unstable, but He makes it unwavering. The "all things that work together for good" become the very things He chooses to bring us near to God. It is in His working that the life and love of God can flow through the valleys that have been carved and cut into our lives by these excruciating circumstances. Those who have come through adversities without fear, confident in the faithfulness of God, are the ones who can be the best towers of strength and sources of inspiration to others who are going through their valleys.

Paul, writing to the Believers in Corinth, seeking to encourage them in their trials, spoke of "the God of all comfort: who comforts us in all our tribulation, that we may be able to comfort them which are in any trouble, by the comfort wherewith we ourselves are comforted of God." Those of us who have experienced God's comfort and sufficiency may encourage others to "dare to believe" God in their trials. God uses our adversities to prepare us to minister to others facing similar difficulties. We need to come alongside of them and share their hurts and travails in the love and compassion of the Lord. May our "valley walk" with the Lord be a refreshing challenge and an encouragement to others, pointing them to the true SOURCE OF OUR STRENGTH, JESUS CHRIST.

The Shepherd's Rod and Staff

"Your rod and your staff they comfort me." Psalm 23:4

A shepherd always carries his "rod and staff," a primary companion and an imperative tool. It is necessary in his care of the sheep. He uses it to discipline the sheep when they get out of line, defend them when they are attacked by dangerous predators, and rescue them from precarious situations. The sheep learn to respect the shepherd's rod and staff. It is a comfort as he uses it to protect them and to guide them in the way they should go.

Ezekiel 20:37 contains a phrase about shepherding: "And I will cause thee to pass under the rod, and I will bring you into the bond of the covenant." How needful this is in our lives, to pass under the rod of God. Why does God use this expression taken from the shepherd's care of the sheep? "That he might bring us into the bond of the covenant." To the shepherd of a flock, the sheep have to "pass under the rod." This is a needful process whereby the shepherd inspects the sheep as they enter the fold for injuries they might have incurred or anything that would be harmful to them. This instills in the sheep a confidence in the shepherd, for they know that this process is for their good and that he is concerned for them. "Your rod and your staff, they comfort me."

The shepherd's "staff" is a long, slender stick with a hook on the end. A shepherd is never without his rod and staff, for he uses it as his primary tool in caring for the sheep. Often he has to reach down into a dangerous place where a sheep has strayed and is caught in a thicket or bush. He takes his staff with its crook on the end and gently lifts the sheep back to safety; then he returns the sheep to the fold.

He uses his staff to guide the sheep in the way he wants them to go. Sheep are very dumb animals and constantly need the directing touch of the staff upon them. How reassuring to sense the Holy Spirit guiding and saying, "This is the way; walk ye in it." How blessed to know the Lord has promised, "Thou wilt show me the path of life: in thy presence is fullness of joy; at thy right hand are pleasures forevermore."

He uses his rod and staff to protect and defend the sheep against the wild animals that would attack them in the pastures. It becomes a defensive tool that the Shepherd uses with great skill and effectiveness. Isaiah spoke of the loving care of the shepherd. "He shall feed his flock like a shepherd: he shall gather the lambs with his arm, and carry them in his bosom, and shall gently lead those that are with young."

As the "rod and staff" comforts the sheep, so may our Good Shepherd, through His Word and the ministry of the Holy Spirit, bring us into an acute consciousness of His presence, protection, and discipline, to guide, defend and comfort us, and to be our strength along the way. Passing under the rod and under His control, we are the "objects of His affection." HOW BLESSED TO HIS OWN IS THE ROD AND STAFF OF OUR GOOD SHEPHERD! "Your rod and your staff they comfort me."

A Table in the Presence of Mine Enemies

"You prepare a table before me in the presence of my enemies: you anoint my head with oil; my cup overflows."
Psalm 23:5

It is a blessed experience to have our lives filled with the joy of the Lord, but even more blessed when the joy and presence of His Spirit overflows from our lives unto others. It is the "overflow" that "spills out of our lives" that blesses, encourages, and challenges others with the glory of His presence in our lives. You might ask, "How do I get to where my cup runs over?" It is the progressive contemplation of His infinite love that overflows our cup.

When we come to the Lord's Table to partake of the communion in remembrance of Him, it is a blessed picture: "You prepare a table before me in the presence of mine enemies." What did He have to go through to prepare this "table of remembrance" for us? Nothing short of His infinite condescending love made possible this solemn communion in which we remember His redeeming sacrifice on Calvary. Can any words express more fully than John 3:16 the love of God and the sacrifice of His Son on Calvary? "For God so loved the world, that he gave his only begotten Son, that whosoever believeth in him shall not perish, but have everlasting life."

When we confess our sin and receive Christ as our Lord and Saviour, He gives us a "seat at the Father's Table." What had to take place for us to have this divine privilege? Paul says, "For he hath made him to be sin for us, who knew no sin; that we might be made the righteousness of God in Him." Such fathomless love, which was subjected to the maximum of man's scorn, rejection, bitterness, hate, blasphemy, and finally the infamy of Calvary, He manifested for sinful mankind. We cannot conceive of such great love; it is beyond our understanding. He went through all of this, "preparing a table in the presence of mine enemies." And then He cried out with a loud voice, "It is finished." What is finished? Our Salvation was made complete by the price He paid in full for our redemption with His Body and Blood on Calvary. Our "table" has been fully prepared and is set before us, filled with the bounties of His mercy and grace! We take our place in humble contrition.

Our heads anointed and our souls filled with the oil of the Holy Spirit, we are seated at the Father's Table. We are lost in the wonder of it all. Our cups overflow with love, adoration, and awe of the greatness of His love, mercy, and grace. Is there a more sacred moment in our Spiritual Journey than when we bow with contrite hearts that have been made pure through His precious blood, gather around His Table, and remember Him, our Lord, our Saviour? How blessed it is to commune with the King of kings and Lord of lords!

Surely, David knew what it meant to "come apart," to sit at His Table in the presence of his enemies, to be freshly anointed with the oil of God, and to rejoice exceedingly with his cup running over! Certainly, we need this refreshing time in His Presence, seated with Him at the table of His grace. THIS IS OUR PRIVILEGED POSITION IN CHRIST!

Goodness and Mercy

"Surely goodness and mercy shall follow me all the days of my life: and I will dwell in the house of the Lord forever." Psalm 23:6

*W*hat a tremendous benediction to this great Psalm. David expresses complete confidence in the faithful hand of God to bring "all things" under the jurisdiction of His love and grace. The Psalmist rests his trust, knowing that the goodness and mercy of God shall follow him like his shadow, all the days of his life. But such a blessing does not end with this life. He says, "I shall dwell in the house of the Lord forever!" Such resignation of heart and soul brings great delight and peace for the present and blessed hope for eternity. This is the privileged care and concern of the Good Shepherd, under which we take our spiritual journey. Can there be two greater companions to accompany us, to embrace us, and to follow us, than His mercy and grace?

Looking at this in retrospect, we are made to realize, as we abide in the Shepherd's care, that no difficulty can arise, no dilemma can emerge, and no seeming disaster can descend on our lives, without it working together for our good and His glory. The confidence of our composure rests in an implicit, unshakable reliance on His ability to do the right thing in any given situation. We can say with Jeremiah, "It is of the Lord's mercies that we are not consumed, because his compassions fail not. They are new every morning: great is thy

175

faithfulness. The Lord is my portion, says my soul, therefore will I hope in Him." God's Mercy withholds all that we deserve because of our sin. God's Grace is the full giving of all He is that we do not deserve, but it is ours because of His great love. To live in the glory of these blessed truths, which are our "constant companions", is to be set free from the bondage of doubt and fear, weakness and weariness, uncertainty and frustration. We rest in His Covenant to us that is secured by the Life of Christ. He is our "Divine Provision", and we draw upon the unfailing resources of His abundant supply.

Is this privileged companionship with the Shepherd to be withheld within the boundaries of my own enjoyment? Is the outflow of His goodness and mercy for me to stop and stagnate in my life? Should not this great blessing be shared with others? Yes, it should. Someone has wisely said, "The only thing we keep in life is what we give away." To harbor the goodness and mercy He showers upon our lives is to withhold all God wants to do through us in sharing His love, so He can live His life freely in us.

What will be the legacy of our life? What qualities of life will we leave behind? Will it be a life of beauty and abundant giving unto others? Will it be a blessing and benediction that will magnify His Name, a peace and contentment, forgiveness and grace, joy and love? Oh that we might leave a legacy to uplift the downtrodden lives of others, being an encouragement in their despair and loneliness, and an inspiration for them to reach out beyond themselves to do the impossible in His strength and blessing. As we are graced with His goodness and mercy, may we share them with all the lives we touch!

His Delight Is in the Law of the Lord

"Blessed is the man who does not walk in the counsel of the wicked or stand in the way of sinners or sit in the seat of mockers. But his delight is in the law of the Lord, and on his law he meditates day and night." Psalm 1:1-2

The order of the day seems to be, "If you want to do it, go for it; everybody's doing it." Few seem to make any effort to control their passions, live by any just standard of truth, or uphold any rational guideline of morals. We are living in a pluralistic society, which is making inroads into our traditional evangelical churches. They proclaim, "It really doesn't make any difference who your god is. There's good in all religions; they all lead to heaven, so worship whatever god pleases you."

Materialism has engulfed our lifestyle to the extent that we think "matter" is the only reality. We should grab all we can get, because "the one who has the most toys wins." It's good to have lots of things, but it's better to have more. Surrounded by the accumulation of things they have sought to make them happy, they find themselves living in a superficial world of materialism, without fulfillment, without God, and without hope.

Another false philosophy making the rounds is "hedonism." The goal of this lifestyle is "pleasure." It is our "moral duty" to obtain gratification in a pleasure-seeking life. Pleasure is paramount, so enjoy as much of it as you can. Solomon sought this approach at the end of his life and found that all such efforts are but vanity, vanity, vanity!

Why do I say all of this (and there are many more such philosophies that people embrace as they seek the "real meaning of life") and why should we be concerned? Because the secular world, under the beguiling influence of Satan, is seeking to redefine our values and undermine the standards of Believers. Followers of these beliefs infiltrate our churches and try to influence Christians to live compromising lives. One destructive thought is to envelope our thinking to "compartmentalize our behavior." Go to church on Sunday, identify with Christians, join in the services rendered, but live as you please the rest of the week – or as soon as you get out of church. Don't expect the truth you have heard to be effective in any way in your life. Simply give a mental assent to what you have heard, and set your own course in life.

Another entrapment is the willingness to "violate our own conscience." We know better, but we act anyway. We "lower the standards" to accommodate our own desires, and the danger increases. We "rationalize" our thinking by comparing our standards to the lives of others. Jeremiah said, "The way of man is not in himself; it is not in man that walks to direct his steps." Our standards, our direction, our way must be found "outside of ourselves" in Jesus Christ, in the Word of God. There is nothing within man to give him a true sense of direction. "Thy Word is a lamp unto thy feet and a light unto thy path." Until we align our hearts to God's Word, we will never find what our soul seeks more than anything else: peace with God and true fulfillment in life, living under His Lordship and the Sovereignty of His will!

Chosen To Be Holy

"He hath chosen us in him before the foundation of the world, that we should be holy and blameless before him in love." Ephesians 1:4

"Holiness of life" is rarely taught and even more rarely understood. Many today shy away from the subject of holiness. Even some Christians view "holiness" as something reserved for "religious fanatics," for people who are not "in tune" with the times or are not living in the reality of today. Basically, the problem is the result of two things. First, they do not know what "holiness" is. Unfortunately, many have seen examples of so-called holy people who were projecting an image that is everything but holy, certainly different than the holy life that Paul describes. Secondly, they are not willing to make the commitment that will result in a holy life.

Holiness of life and character is the outward display of the in-living Christ. It displays the virtues of righteousness that God implants in us as a "new creation in Christ." It is surrendering the control of our life and will to His Lordship. Holiness is found in the Christian who has been "renewed in the Spirit of their mind," whose thoughts, desires, and decisions will manifest His Abounding Love to all. Their whole outlook on life, their motives, their very method of thinking, their attitudes and priorities, are founded upon a Godly perspective. They live under the Sovereign Control of God. This should be the "most reasonable thing we can do." (Romans 12:1, 2)

To this end "we have been chosen in Him" before the foundation of the world. God has not "requested" that we be holy; He has commanded us to be so. "Be ye holy, for I am holy." Is there anything as effective, as powerful, as fruitful as a life lived in the power of the Holy Spirit and displaying before all a life of righteousness and holiness?

Dr. Raymond Edman, in his booklet *"How They Were Won,"* gives a brief account of John Bunyan, the author of *"Pilgrim's Progress."* He was won to Christ because two people embraced the grace and command of God "to live holy and righteously in the power of the Holy Spirit." Bunyan was a man of such degradation, drunkenness, and despicable character that he was known as an "outcast from society." He was so debauched before his conversion that he could neither read nor write. He married a poor girl who knew "something" about Christ, and they lived in abject poverty. At night she would read *"Foxe's Book of Martyrs,"* about holy men who paid for their faith with their lives. Through his loving wife and "Holy Mr. Gifford," the pastor of the small church in Bedford who reached out in godly love to the "meanest man in town," John Bunyan accepted Christ as Lord and Saviour. The Holy Spirit transformed the "derelict of humanity," who spent 12 years in jail as a result of his intense preaching. While there, God opened up his life to write of his "spiritual warfare" in his 29th book, *"Pilgrim's Progress,"* a worldwide bestseller, second only to the Bible. The effects of John Bunyan's life are inestimable. Millions have come to Christ through his writings, because God's Hand was upon two humble Christians who dared to live lives of "holiness" and reached out in love to one in desperate need. Oh that we might "live the life to which we have been called"! "He hath chosen us, that we should be holy and blameless before Him I love."

The Hairs of Your Head

"But the very hairs of your head are numbered." Matthew 10:30

We acknowledge the "providence of God" without difficulty, but when we apply the same principle of faith to "specifics," we find discrepancies within the framework of our faith. This is incompatible. Your faith must stand true in every measure of testing as to the "providence of God." Its foundation must be our concept of the Majesty of God, "Who He Is" in all of His Greatness. The Psalmist said, "His greatness is unsearchable, beyond understanding, fathomless. His knowledge, who can know it." Let me ask you, "How great is your God?" When David meditated upon the vast expanse of God's creation, the fathomless might and power of God, that by Him all things were created, consist, and are held together, he cried out, "What is man that thou art mindful of him?" When we have the right concept of His Majesty, is there anything we might encounter that He does not have full control and authority over, that He cannot enable us to be more than conquerors?

Consider the "providence of God" in the life of Moses. He was left in the bulrushes of the water, found by the King's daughter, brought up and trained in royalty, but chosen of God "in His providence" to lead His people out of bondage to Canaan. Consider Job, subjected to the scourging of Satan himself, enduring the suffering as no other man, yet how greatly his happiness was increased after

181

his affliction. Often the loss of our temporal happiness will be more than counterbalanced by our spiritual prosperity. Consider Joseph, despised by his brothers, thrown into a pit to die, sold to foreigners, falsely accused, imprisoned, BUT GOD, in "His divine providence," was preparing him to reign second only to the King, and to be the instrument to save his family.

The finite limitation of our "sight" creates the problem. We need to walk more by faith and less by sight, more by our "trust in an Almighty God" than leaning upon the "faulty understanding of our own mind." Jesus said unto Martha, "Said I not unto thee, that if thou would believe, you should see the glory of God?" We would do well to heed the words of Isaiah: "Who is among you that fears the Lord, that obeys the voice of his servant, that walks in darkness and hath no light? Let him trust in the name of the Lord, and stay upon his God." Oh that we might learn in the "providence of God", His wisdom, His power, His love, His faithfulness, as we observe the "ways of God, which are past finding out." This was the experience of the widow of Zarephath when her son was raised from death. She exclaimed to Elijah, "Now I KNOW that His Word is true!" Or as Job, "I have heard thee by the hearing of the ear, but NOW mine eye sees thee." David said after emerging out of temporal affliction, "Many shall see it and fear, and shall trust in the Lord." The knowledge we have of God and Christ is mere "theory" until we have learned the same by our own personal experience. When our faith is confirmed by actual experience, then it is as convincing as sight itself.

See His Hand in everything, guiding us in His loving, providential care for our good and His glory, that in all things He might be magnified and we might be "conformed unto His image." "Is there anything He cannot do for him that believeth?"

There Is no Restraint to the Lord

"Come, let us go over to the garrison of these uncircumcised: it may be that the Lord will work for us: for there is no restraint to the Lord to save by many or by few." 1 Samuel 14:6

Hudson Taylor, the great pioneer missionary to Inland China, said, "There are no circumstances so great that we do not need His Grace, nor are there any circumstances so desperate that His Grace is not All Sufficient." "God hath raised us up together and made us to sit together in heavenly places in Christ Jesus." Have you claimed "your seat" at the Father's Table? The riches of His grace are spread before you and are "yours to appropriate by faith," which He has purchased for you. God delights to magnify His Strength in the weakness of His people, to intercede for them in the most devastating circumstances, and to make a way of deliverance when there is no way. Is it not the reason "He thus waits" until we are reduced to our lowest extremities; until we get to the end of our way, our strength, our ability, our resources, and our attitude in thinking "we" can handle our problem? Peter said, "Cast all your anxieties upon Him, for He cares for you." It is then that His grace becomes our portion and we rest in Him. Why does it take us so long to reach that point?

Look at Jonathan's victory over the Philistines. God stirred the heart of Jonathan and his armourbearer to attack a garrison of Philistines, when nothing but utter destruction and defeat stood starkly before them. Humanly speaking, this was an impossible task, even by a considerable force. They cast themselves upon the Lord and let Him decide what they should do, and God answered their faith. In spite of the sharp rocks they had to ascend, the hopeless task before them, exposed in open daylight to the enemy, and the mockery they endured, they realized that THE BATTLE WAS THE LORD'S.

This account of Jonathan and his armor bearer is inferior to few, either in the strangeness of its feats or the magnitude of the victory. God used TWO MEN, full of faith, committed unreservedly to Him, to rout a Philistine army of thousands. "If God be for us, who can be against us?" The weakest of men "with God" is greater than an army of thousands of men "without Him."

What was the focus of Jonathan and his armor bearer? Was it the enemy with their thousands and all their warring weapons? NOT AT ALL. Their focus and faith were on the Mighty God of Abraham, Isaac, and Jacob. Two things encompassed Jonathan as he faced the enemy: "There is no restraint to the Lord to save, whether by many or by few," and his faith, "It may be that the Lord will work for us." Our Strength is the Lord, who is the Object of our faith!

In dependence upon God, we should go forth, fearing nothing, being "strong in the Lord and in the power of His might." We should gird on the armor and go forth with our sling and five stones against every enemy, not doubting, but in full faith. We shall see that like Goliath, he too shall fall before us. God has already gained the victory for us. It is ours to claim by faith. Let us "dare to believe" with unrelenting trust and see the mighty Hand of God remove the mountains, part the sea, and triumph over our enemy!

The Lord Is With Thee

"And the angel of the Lord appeared unto him, and said unto him, The Lord is with thee, thou mighty man of valour." Judges 6:12

"And the children of Israel did evil in the sight of the Lord, and the Lord delivered them into the hand of Midian seven years." A very short but conclusive and definite judgment of Israel. They simply did not follow God's word, so they suffered the consequences of their own choice. Now, they were under the bondage and oppression of the Midianites and Amalekites. For seven years they came at harvest time and took all their grain "and left no sustenance for Israel, neither sheep, nor ox, nor donkey" and sought to destroy the land. They cried unto the Lord, and He sent a prophet, who told them the many times God had delivered them and how they had disobeyed God. Now, "The Angel of the Lord appeared unto him [Gideon] and said unto him, "The Lord is with thee, thou mighty man of valour." Gideon took issue with the angel because of their oppression. "The Lord turned to him and said, go in the strength you have and save Israel out of Midian's hand. Am I not sending you?" "If God be for us, who can be against us?"

Gideon took issue, not with what God was, but with what he was; not what God could do, but with what he might do. We fall into the same pattern. It's not who we are, what we have, or what we can do, but altogether who 'God' is, what 'He' has, and what 'He'

185

can do. "It's not by might nor by power, but by my Spirit, says the Lord." Gideon prepared for battle. He built an altar unto the Lord and tore down the altar to Baal. If we are going to be effective in our testimony, we must destroy everything that will hinder the full working of the Holy Spirit in our lives. Gideon offers a burnt offering unto the Lord. This signifies the complete surrender of his will and his entire devotion to the Lord. When the enemy rose up against Israel, "Then the Spirit of the Lord came upon Gideon." He gathered his army. Gideon would soon see that God's power is mightier than a host of men.

Now God comes on the scene. Gideon gathered 32,000 men. God said, "That's too many." Those who were afraid (22,000) were sent home. God put the rest to a test, and 9,700 were sent home. Only 300 were left! Why do you think God reduced his army down to 300 men? So they would experience the Mighty Power of God and realize HE was the One they should trust for victory. But how did they prepare for battle? God armed them not with shield and sword, but with a Pitcher, a Lamp, a Trumpet, and a Battle Cry. When they executed God's Plan, panic struck the enemy and they destroyed themselves! What application is in this for us?

Draw back from nothing to which we are called. Undertake nothing in our own strength. Go forth confident of His leading. Doubt nothing in which God has promised His help. Take no glory for what God does for us. Exercise unwavering faith in an Omnipotent God. The Holy Spirit is seizing upon and using for God's glory those that are of a "broken and contrite spirit." That which will stand the judgment fire of eternity will not be what "we" have done, but what "HE" has done through us!

Stand Fast

"Therefore, brethren, stand fast, and hold to the traditions which ye have been taught, whether by word, or our epistle."
2 Thessalonians 2:15

*P*aul had gained the confidence and love of the Christians in the church at Thessalonica as he had ministered among them. He taught them the Truth and many had believed. There was a growth in grace evidenced by their exceeding faith, their abounding love for God and one another, and their patience in the midst of cruel trials and persecutions. Now it was time for them to stand fast, to hold on, and to "dig in" to what they had been taught.

One of the beautiful characteristics of Paul's letters to the churches is how he expresses his "concern" for them, his "interest: in them, his "joy" over them, and his "life of prayer" on their behalf. They were dear to his heart and brothers in Christ. He often says they are bound together with a "bond of the love of God," and in verse 13 refers to being "loved by the Lord." This word "loved" combines two aspects of an action: something that occurred in the past, and something that continues into the present. As these Believers reflected on this dual significance of God's love, it would take them back to His redeeming love when they received Christ as their Saviour. It also reminded them that God's love for them continues undiminished and uninterrupted to the present time. They could be confident that they would continue to be the objects of His Divine Love. When Moses led the people of Israel through the Red Sea, delivering them from their enemy, he set up an Altar of Remembrance and called it Ebenezer, which means "Hitherto Hath The Lord Helped Us." Whenever children asked their parents what the altar meant, the parents would tell them of God's faithfulness in delivering them from the Egyptians. Paul, in challenging these Christians to "stand fast," is saying as Moses said unto Israel, "REMEMBER ALL THE WAY GOD HAS LED YOU." From what we have received HITHERTO, we may claim by faith all that is HENCEFORTH. Let me remind you of just a few.

In times we need COMFORT, Psalm 18:2: "The Lord is my rock, and my fortress, and my deliverer; my God, my strength in whom I will trust; my buckler, and the horn of my salvation, and my high tower."

In times of FEAR, Isaiah 43:1-3: "Fear not: for I have redeemed you, I have called you by your name; you are mine. When you pass through the waters, I will be with you; and through the rivers, they shall not overflow you; when you walk through the fire, you shall not be burned; neither shall the flame kindle you. For I am the Lord your God."

In times of TROUBLE, Psalm 32:7: "You are my hiding place; you shall preserve me in trouble; you will compass me about with songs of deliverance."

In times we need GUIDIANCE, Isaiah 42:16: "And I will bring the blind by the way that they knew not; I will lead in paths that they have not known: I will make darkness light before them, and crooked ways straight. These things I will do unto them, and not forsake them."

Let us thank Him for all the way "He has led us" and trust Him for all the way "that is before us." From all we have received HITHERTO, let us claim by faith all that is HENCEFORTH. He is faithful that promised. STAND FAST!

God Pre-eminent in All Things

"You shall have no other gods before me." Exodus 20:3

Unbelievers refer to the Ten Commandments as rigid and to God as a stern taskmaster in the giving of the law when He said, "Thou shall not" do this or that. If God has in His heart only rigid requirements and prohibitive desires for mankind, we would have to say He is a God of Law. Where are mercy and grace? Ah, but if we want to see what God is like, we only have to look at Jesus Christ on Calvary's Cross, full of Grace and Truth manifesting Unconditional Love. "For in Him dwells all the fullness of the Godhead bodily." (Colossians 2:9)

The Law was given as God's "standard" of what man ought to be, and reveals the sinfulness of man. It is like a mirror that reflects man's moral derangement. It is like a plumb line beside a bowed wall; it reveals crooked lines. It is like a bright light; it reveals hindrances in the way. But it does not create evil, nor is it capable of correcting it; it simply reveals what's there. That which can only curse, can never justify. That which can only kill, can never be a rule to live by. The Law is neither the "ground of life" for the sinner or the "rule of life" for the Believer. The Gospel of grace gives life as the "only proper ground" of forgiveness.

What do you think God means when He says, "Thou shall have no other gods before me."? Do you immediately think of idols or icons that people revere or worship? It goes deeper than that. It means, "giving honor, reverence, or glory to any creature or creation, which is due to God only." Now, let's be very practical. What are some of the "gods" that confront us? How about pride, covetousness, sensuality, ego, pleasure, or whatever is esteemed or loved, feared or served, delighted in or depended on, more than God? That becomes our god and is idolatry.

God said, "My people have committed two sins. They have forsaken me, the fountain of living waters, and hewed them out cisterns, broken cisterns, that hold no water." What is it in creation that is not a product of His power and a gift of His grace? That which satisfies the heart and soul of man finds its Source from His grace and love. What does He require of us? He requires us to "regard Him" as the Source of Life and true joy, "acknowledge Him" in all we have and do, and "delight in Him" as our Friend, our Father, and our Everlasting Portion. But what do we prefer? We prefer pleasure, fame, fortune, power, and the world's acclaim. Sin is making these things the "chief pursuits" of our lives, letting them draw us away from God, letting them claim the affection that is due to God alone. God refers to such attitudes and conduct as "forsaking the fountain of living waters." God said, "Hearken diligently unto me, and eat ye that which is good, and let your soul delight itself in fatness." He is the "fountainhead" from which all the refreshing, living waters find their source. So come, "that out of your innermost being shall flow rivers of living water. The water that I shall give him shall be in him a well of water, springing up into everlasting life!" Make Christ pre-eminent in the whole of your life. He is Lord, to be revered above all.

Do Not Steal Time With God

"And God spoke all these words, saying, I am the Lord thy God, which brought thee out of the land of Egypt, out of the house of bondage...Thou shalt not steal." Exodus 20:1, 2, 15

*A*part from life itself, what is the most important thing we have to deal with? It is TIME. Our economy is valued in time; the wages we get paid are in relation to our ability and the time we spend exercising that ability. Time is a very important commodity. As Christians, we have a responsibility to invest our time wisely for His glory. But how do we spend our TIME?

We steal time by squandering it aimlessly in the pursuit of meaningless desires and pleasure of the flesh. How often we have said to ourselves after some event or occasion, "What a waste of time." We realize we have not spent our TIME wisely.

We steal time that God has set for the development and maturing of our lives. Athletes spend countless hours, months, and years for a special event or for their participation in sports. Their whole life centers upon the "honing of their skills" to the maximum. When the "time of opportunity" comes, they are ready. So God seeks to bring us to "spiritual maturity" through the process of "conforming us to the image of His Son." We must not shrink from the TIME needed to prepare and mature us.

We steal time from the opportunities God sends our way that may never come again. We need to be an encouragement to those who are in despair, lonely, and in need of someone to "come alongside of them and let them know we care." TIME to encourage others!

We steal time God has given us to feed upon His Word in meditation, in studying the Scriptures, in letting God speak to us intimately and personally. We need to spend time in prayer, communing with Him, and lifting up our hearts in praise, adoration, and worship. We need time for God to respond and reveal Himself to us. TIME with God!

We steal time from the process of faith that God wants to instill in our hearts. Through our adversities, God wants to deepen and stretch our faith so it will be securely anchored in HIM. When we read of Paul's lifelong encounters with suffering, trials, beatings, shipwreck, hunger, and persecution, and his being cast down, distressed, perplexed, some may ask, "Was that like a God of infinite power that was in control of his life?" Yes, it was just like the Lord! TIME when God is working!

He was molding Paul's life to be the great man of God "he was to become." What was Paul's response? He rises above all his adversities and says, "But thanks be unto God, who always leads us in triumphal procession in Christ and through us spreads everywhere the fragrance of the knowledge of him, for we are unto God the aroma of Christ." Can anything compare to such workings of His grace in our lives that we may "become unto God the aroma of Christ among those who are being saved and those who are perishing"? TIME when we are becoming like Him!

When the Lord was Sovereign in Paul's life, severe conflicts immediately came, which were always persistent and never ended. Perplexed, but not in despair; persecuted, but not forsaken; cast down, but not destroyed; he "always emerged victorious" through Jesus Christ! TIME WITH GOD IS IMPERATIVE if we are to grow in grace and be "conformed to the image of His Son."

Keep the Way of the Lord

"For I know him, that he will command his children and his household after him, and they shall keep the way of the Lord to do justice and judgment." Genesis 18:19

*T*he commitment of Abraham's life to God and his subsequent life of faith were outgrowths of "walking with God." After God called him to leave his country and to go where He would lead him, faith characterized his whole life. God had so impacted his heart that no attraction of this world had any consideration in Abraham's journey. When God said to Abraham, "I know him," I think He reviewed the whole of Abraham's life and character, and came to some of the following conclusions:

I know his PRINCIPLE. He regards all that he possesses – his wisdom, his power, his influence, and his family – as gifts for the good of others and for the glory of My Name. He recognizes the ONE who is the Source of his Strength and will govern his life under the Sovereignty of God.

I know his INCLINATION. He has a zeal for my honor. He longs to be a channel of blessing and to exalt and magnify My Name. He has a love for others and a desire to benefit them in every way possible to his utmost ability. He derives great satisfaction from being a blessing to them.

I know his PRACTICE. He is faithful in uniting his family to read the Word and pray, applying the Truth and principles of my commandments to their lives. He seeks to lead them in worship and in serving Me, teaching them reverence, responsibility, and respect.

I know his INNER HEART. He enters into all things as one who feels his responsibility and has but one desire, to approve himself to Me. He seeks to walk before men in a godly manner so as to glorify Me. He desires to be influenced by Me before he seeks to influence others.

I know his FAITH. When I call upon him, he will respond without question, debate, or hesitancy. He will follow with his eyes fixed on Me, even though he knows not where I might lead him. He will put his unreserved trust in Me. I will be the focus of his walk and life.

God saw these characteristics and many more in His servant Abraham. Wouldn't it be wonderful if God "knew us" in such a measure of devotedness and commitment? Abraham was not satisfied with simply giving good advice to his children; "he commanded them." He maintained authority over his family and exercised that authority and responsibility before God. His godly authority demanded respect, his discipline established character, and his godly character was a role model to his family and all he came in contact with. Abraham's life was lived "outside the confinement of himself." He was controlled by One, even God Himself, who was from "without," who led him, empowered him, revealed Himself to him, and walked with him. Abraham was known as "a friend of God." Look closely at Abraham's life and see the sterling qualities that embraced him. How dramatically these qualities were manifested when he told Lot to choose whatever land he desired, although this was rightfully his choice. He left his choice in the hands of God, and afterward God said, "Look [in all directions] at all of this I will give to you and your descendants." Oh that we might so surrender our heart and life to His Sovereign control and Lordship.

Your Faith Has Healed You

"She said to herself, 'If I only touch his cloak, I will be healed.' Jesus turned and saw her. 'Take heart, daughter,' he said. 'Your faith has healed you.' And the woman was healed from that moment. Matthew 9:21, 22

We have read, "Without faith, it is impossible to please God." How do we apply such a statement to the reality of everyday living? Let's ask it another way. Are we pleasing God in our everyday life by applying faith in all we are doing? I think we must now ask, "What is faith and how do we apply it?" Now, this can stretch into a very long and complicated discussion, but let's confine it to a simple explanation and application for the purpose of this devotion.

Simply put, faith is our unutterable trust in God. Trust in One whose character is infallible, who tests our trust in Him so that it can be turned into a personal possession. It is our unwavering reliance upon His choosing. Not what's good for us, a choice that would be influenced by common sense, but what is "best and glorifying to Him." It is not sentiment, but a vigorous confidence built on the fact that God is holy love. It is a reckless confidence in God, a supernatural relationship born of God, with which He seeks to clothe our lives so that they become glorious opportunities for seeing His supernatural power manifested in the normal routine of our daily living. His life lived through us.

Such was the experience of the needy woman who had been afflicted for 12 years with an "issue of blood." There was nothing within her to command any action on the part of Jesus, except her "complete abandonment and unutterable trust" in Jesus Christ, that He was able to supernaturally heal her. She recognized in Christ a "holy love" that would reach the depths of her human need. By His Divine power, He could "do exceeding abundantly above all she could ask or think." So, what happened? She exercised complete trust in Him and was fully delivered from her desperate need. Now, there is a fine point here we need to understand. There is a difference between "belief" and "trust." Belief is when we acknowledge a truth, or a standard of knowledge, a creed, or a principle. That's good in itself, but it falls far short in the "reality of daily life" when we are in great distress. Trust is when we "commit what we believe by applying it to active circumstances." This reflects a personal possession of what we believe. It is putting into practice the principles of our faith.

James makes it very clear when he says, "A man may say, you have faith and I have works: show me your faith without your works, and I will show you my faith by my works. You believe that there is one God; you do well: the devils also believe, and tremble. But will you know, O vain man, that faith without works is dead?" We find many today who adhere intellectually to truth, principles of faith, creeds, tradition, and forms of worship, but have never put their "unutterable trust in the Truth" or abandoned themselves to the One who is "the Way, the Truth, and the Life." This woman "activated her belief with irrevocable trust in Jesus Christ," and He said, "Your faith hath made you whole!" Such childlike faith in Almighty God brings deliverance, a walk with the Lord that is undeniable, where He does the impossible! "Dare to Believe" in the Majesty of God!

Ye Shall Receive Power

"But ye shall receive power, after that the Holy Ghost is come upon you: and ye shall be witnesses unto me both in Jerusalem, and in all Judea, and in Samaria, and unto the uttermost part of the earth." Acts 1:8

The disciples had been intimately associated with Jesus for three years, witnessing His miracles and sitting under His profound teaching. Yet, when He spoke to them of His death, His resurrection, His ascension, of going back to the Father, and of preparing a place for them, they were completely bewildered. When He told them He would send to them a Comforter who would more than compensate for the loss of His bodily presence with them, they were beside themselves. They were fearful, timid, ill prepared, unstable, and not willing to be identified with Him. At the crucifixion, where were all His disciples? After their intimate experience, when He washed their feet as the Servant of Jehovah, they followed Him to Gethsemane, but fled at the sign of the Cross.

But then He tells them to tarry in Jerusalem and wait for the gift my Father hath promised. You will receive power when the Holy Ghost comes on you. In simple obedience they were to wait. We read, "And all of these, with their minds in full agreement, devoted themselves steadfastly to prayer." Three things are paramount in these few words and are so essential to our lives: They had "unity of spirit, they devoted themselves to hear from God, and they sought

197

God in prevailing prayer." Nothing takes the place of being in His Presence in prayer, and receiving the anointing and power of the Holy Spirit for whatever task God gives us to do. Most assuredly, this we need to do, that we might walk worthy of Him day by day.

The coming of the Comforter meant the "indwelling and abiding presence" of the Lord Jesus Christ Himself, as an Ever Present, All Sufficient, Everlasting Saviour. He would now, by the indwelling of the Holy Spirit in their lives, be able to minister to their needs, hear their prayers, and manifest His Presence and Power to everyone at the same time. No longer limited by His bodily presence, He now "indwells" each Believer.

Through the Holy Spirit, He imparts to us His very Life and feeds us with the Living Bread. He breathes into us His Peace that passes our understanding. He sheds abroad in our hearts the Love of God. He meets our needs according to His riches in glory. He reveals unto us an understanding of His Word. He pours into our lives the fullness of His resurrected life. He renews our strength by ministering to our inner man by the might of His power. All of this, and infinitely more, could never have been possible if Jesus had not ascended to the Father. He sent unto us the Indwelling Presence of the Holy Spirit. Paul writes, "Don't you know that you yourselves are God's temple, and that God's Spirit lives in you?" This is the secret of a victorious life. It is when the fullness of the Holy Spirit occupies the whole of our life with the adequacy of Christ. It is when He, Who is our Life, lives freely and fully through us. It is the out-living of the in-living Christ. We must be emptied of self and free from continual sin, which impedes the work of grace He wants to do in our lives, whether in service or in our daily walk. It must be HIS LIFE LIVED THROUGH US!

Worship God in the Spirit

"Beware of the concision. For we are the circumcision, which worship God in the Spirit, and rejoice in Christ Jesus, and have no confidence in the flesh." Philippians 3:2,3

*T*hroughout our churches, we find not only varied forms of customs, creeds, and traditions that comprise "worship" to many, but also an expanded concept of worship by those who form the body of worshippers. What characterizes a "true" worshipper? What is the attitude of our heart when we come to worship the Lord? How does our everyday life testify to the faith we proclaim? Are any of these things important to you as a professing Christian? They are more important than you realize!

Paul was concerned with all of these questions. Just before revealing the tremendous testimony of his background to the Believers, God's work of grace in his life, and the new focus of his heart and life, he pointedly reminded them, "Be aware of the concision." Who were they? They were distinctly different; they were evil-workers, mutilators of the flesh. Paul says, "We are the circumcision." God had made a Covenant with Abraham, and the sign and seal of that Covenant was "circumcision." It was evidence of a special relationship the people of Israel had with God. That was a sign identifying them as God's Chosen People.

Unfortunately, the people of Israel were well known for their physical circumcision, but many lacked the "circumcision of their spiritual lives." They were very technical in the religious observance of circumcision, but very lax and indifferent to the "spiritual circumcision", the reality of having their hearts and lives separated from all that was displeasing to God. It was, as we see in so many churches today: "Religion Without Reality" and "Ritual Without Response." It was "Creeds Without Confession" and a "Form of Worship" denying the Power thereof.

Paul said, "We are the circumcision which worship God in the Spirit and rejoice in Christ Jesus, and have no confidence in the flesh." Among the professed Believers in Philippi, Paul saw many who were zealous advocates of the externals of religion, while altogether destitute of its life and the Power of God that radically changes lives from within. It was not "life" produced by their efforts or observances of creeds, customs, or traditions, but FAITH IN THE LIVING CHRIST. It is the result of recognizing our totally lost condition as a sinner before a holy God and receiving Christ as our Saviour. It is then that the Believer recognizes the "true significance" of the customs, forms, and traditions of worship that exist "to magnify the Lord and exalt Him" in His rightful place, not to take the place of our Lord Jesus Christ, who is the sole object of our affection and worship. They are not the "props of a professing faith," but channels by which we recognize more fully the place He occupies on the Throne of our Hearts. Jesus Christ is the One sitting at the right hand of the Father, "high and lifted up," to Whom we bow in reverential praise and worship, and cry out with the seraphims, "Holy, holy, holy is the Lord of hosts: the whole earth is full of his glory!" Let not the "concision" confuse, change, alter, or affect the true commitment of your heart to Christ by persuading you to put your confidence in the flesh. WE WORSHIP GOD IN AND BY THE SPIRIT. We exult and glory in Christ Jesus, Our Lord and Saviour! It is He who is to be magnified and exalted!

In the Days When the Judges Ruled

"Now it came to pass in the days when the judges ruled, that there was a famine in the land. And a certain man of Bethlehem-Judah went to sojourn in the country of Moab, he, and his wife, and his two sons." Ruth 1:1

It's striking to me how God's Word says so much in so few words. "In the days when the judges ruled" has volumes to say of all that took place during those dark days when Israel turned from God to idolatry and sin. Israel would "reel to and fro, and stagger like a drunken man, and are at their wits' end." Then they would "cry unto the Lord and He would bring them out of their distresses." There were repeated failures and departures from God. Time and again, God sent a famine as a customary method of judgment. There was no consistent commitment or dedication to God!

In these times of great need, Elimelech decided to leave Bethlehem-Judah and go to the country of Moab. Bethlehem-Judah means "house of bread and praise," which suggests God's presence and provision. Elimelech was a member of the Tribe of Judah and one of God's chosen people. But now he made a choice to leave the wonderful house of the Father and to go to the "far country" of Moab, because of the famine in the land. The famine "struck terror" in the heart of Elimelech, but not "unwavering trust" in God. There is always trouble for the prodigal son in the "far country." Better to trust God in the famine, than to dwell in the far country with its food "without God."

We are reminded of the prodigal son who, like Elimelech, left his father's house of plenty, took his inheritance, and dwelt in the "far country." It was there, away from God, they both had "tears of sorrow" instead of "tears of joy" in Bethlehem. The same thing took place with Abraham. God called him out of Ur of the Chaldees and instructed him to dwell in Canaan. Then we read, "There was a famine in the land; and Abraham went down into Egypt to sojourn there." Anytime we leave the place of blessing and stray from His Presence, it is always a "downward path" that is never delightful, but is devastating, destructive, and ends in tragedy. God had given no instructions to Abraham to leave the Land of Promise, but the constant trek of multitudes passing before his tent, migrating to the land of Egypt, was too much for Abraham. He silently folded his tent, joined the crowd, and journeyed to Egypt.

It was in the land of Egypt, the "far country," that Abraham, like Elimelech and the Prodigal Son, acquired all his future trouble. He became wealthy and took an Egyptian maid, which contributed to his undoing. Notice that while Abraham dwelt in Egypt, God did not appear to him. When he returned, God immediately communicated with him.

All three of these men left the "place of blessing" to seek refuge in a "far country." All three saw the dilemma of their decision. Abraham and the Prodigal Son experienced the exceeding goodness and grace of God in returning to intimacy with the Father. How clear the message is to us! Dare to trust God "in" the time of need, "in" our difficulty, "in" our distress, and you will find Him ever faithful, Our Refuge, Our Hiding Place, and Our Sure Foundation. He will be OUR SUFFICIENCY FOR EVERY NEED, OUR EVER-PRESENT HELP!

They Continued Steadfastly

"And they continued steadfastly in the apostles' doctrine and fellowship, and breaking of bread, and in prayers." Acts 2:42

The disciples and the others who were gathered in the "upper room" had just experienced being "filled with the Holy Ghost." Jerusalem was filled with devout men from every nation under heaven, and they were all amazed as they heard these men of God speaking in their own language. Peter seizes this unique gathering and begins to preach unto them. You need to notice that this tremendous gathering was composed of many who only days had before railed at Christ, and were shouting "Crucify Him, crucify Him," and were responsible for His crucifixion. When Peter finished his sermon, "They were pricked in their heart, and said to Peter and the rest of the apostles, Men and brethren, what shall we do? And Peter said unto them, repent, and be baptized every one of you in the name Jesus Christ for the remission for your sins. And there were added unto them 3,000 souls." Can you imagine the reaction Peter must have had?

What an amazing manifestation of the power of God! These new Believers were staunch enemies of Christ and everything the Apostles stood for. Their hate had turned to love, their animosity had turned to contrition, their pride had turned to humility, and their anger had been replaced with the peace of God. Their desire to disrupt and destroy had become a determination to share, not only their possessions but also their lives in a "unity of spirit and a love one to another." Only the Holy Spirit could have accomplished this. What an incredible scene! This was truly a MIRACLE! God had come upon this gathering and worked in the hearts of both the Apostles and these new Believers, and had turned their relationship to "unconditional love" for each other and for God. Wow! What a sight! Broken in heart, with tears of repentance, confession of soul, and embraces of love, they were receptive and responsive to the Holy Spirit drawing them unto God.

Four things followed that confirmed the sincerity of their faith: They continued steadfastly in the Apostles' teachings, they continued daily with one accord in fellowship, they gathered together in the breaking of bread, and they devoted themselves to prayer. What a remarkable transformation took place in the lives of these new Believers. Here were enemies of Christ now coming into the "very Presence of God," laying bare their hearts in prayer, praise, and thanksgiving for the work of grace, which radically changed their life! Did you know the same thing is taking place today in lives that are open to God's mercy and grace?

I'm sure Peter, along with the other Apostles, prayed for these new Believers that they might see the "full range of their redemption" and the "full measure of God's grace." Listen to Paul's prayer for them: "I keep asking that the God of our Lord Jesus Christ, the glorious Father, may give you the spirit of wisdom and revelation, so that you may know Him better. I pray also that the 'eyes of your heart may be enlightened,' in order that you may 'know the hope to which He has called you,' the 'riches of His glorious inheritance' in the saints, and 'His incomparable great power' for us who believe." Oh that we might respond with openness of heart and soul, as those new Believers did, and seek to live and serve in the power of the Holy Spirit where God's Love prevails and abounds.

The Fire of the Lord Fell

"Then the fire of the Lord fell, and consumed the burnt sacrifice, and the wood, and the stones, and the dust, and licked up the water that was in the trench." 1 Kings 18:38

*E*lijah was a great man who exemplified extraordinary faith and effective prayer. There are four remarkable instances in his life of the efficacy of the fervent prayer of a righteous man.

He prayed for the restoration of the widow's son at Zarephath, and the child was restored to life.

He prayed earnestly that it would not rain, and it rained not on the earth for three and a half years.

He prayed at Mt. Carmel when he confronted the 450 Priests of Baal to contest who was the true and living God, and "the fire of the Lord" fell and consumed the sacrifice, proving to these idolatrous people that He was the true God.

After the miraculous victory, he prayed that God again would bring rain upon the scorched earth, and the rain fell in abundance.

After the "fire of the Lord fell," we need to notice something very significant. God's power was miraculously manifested, and the people shouted, "The Lord, He is God". You would have thought that this inferred, "If He is the True and Living God, He shall be our God, and we will serve Him only." I'm sure there were some who believed and committed their lives to Him. However, numbers of these people were only convinced, not CONVERTED. They did not yield to the truth that He was the Only True God, nor consent to the covenant He gave to all who believed in Him. The "miracle of the moment" had impressed them, even Ahab, but their "hearts were not changed." No true faith had taken possession of them! Today, those who are drawn to an awakening of their sins are not the only ones who refuse to respond; the Believers, who are drawn by the Holy Spirit to a deeper commitment to the Lord, often do not yield. They, too, are impressed and convinced by the Truth, but they choose their own preferences instead of His.

Then, after the glorious victory, Elijah goes to the top of Mt. Carmel to converse with God. In humility of spirit and contrition of heart, we find the secret of Elijah's greatness. It was his utter dependence upon God, recognizing he is but a "channel" through which God would manifest His power. What happens in our seasons of "true" prayer? Our corrupt nature is revealed by His holiness. Our hearts are most thoroughly broken before Him, and the remains of self-love are effectively demolished. The Word cleanses our hearts, and the "channel" is made ready to be used by Him. We are prepared by the Holy Spirit to receive the seed of the Word. The fountain of truth is laid deep and implanted in our soul, and when God answers our prayer, great is our joy! We recognize anew that it is the Lord's doing, not ours!

In the same measure that we "prevail in prayer," we will be made "strong and steadfast" in our spiritual walk and "effective and fruitful" in our outreach to others. God said, "Come boldly to the throne of grace, that you might obtain mercy and find grace to help in time of need." What an inconceivable, blessed privilege we have of coming into His very presence! Oh that we would avail ourselves more often of His Throne, baring our souls before the Lord of lords and Kings of kings!

You Shall Not Covet

"I am the Lord your God, who brought you out of the land
of Egypt, out of the land of slavery...You shall not covet."
Exodus 20:2, 17

To deal with this command by God, "You shall not covet",
we need to understand what it means to covet. Covetousness
deals with an inward, mental process associated with motivation and
desire, which, if left unchecked, leads to sinful actions and dreadful
circumstances. It can consume a person. It leads to greed and makes
us determined to have more, whatever the cost and by whatever the
means. Our eyes are focused upon the "gratification of our gain"
rather than on the "consequences of our sin" in getting it. We ignore
completely that God knows and sees all we do, and that He will
justly reward our evil ways. "Your sin will find you out."

An example of this is seen when the people of Israel, under
Joshua, attacked the small village of Ai. God had miraculously
given them victory over Jericho. Joshua had explicitly followed
God's plan in conquering Jericho, but when he saw the small village
of Ai, he was convinced he could do this "on his own." What a
humbling awakening awaited him. Israel enjoyed the "spoils" of the
battle at Jericho, but God told Joshua "nothing" was to be taken
from Ai. When his men returned from a surprising defeat, Joshua
was devastated. How could this happen? Then God rebuked Joshua.
"Get thee up; wherefore liest thou thus upon thy face? Israel hath

sinned." Israel had disobeyed God! What happened? One soldier, Achan, coveted a Babylonian garment, along with some gold and silver. One obscure individual, one simple act of sin, one look of covetousness, stopped the course of a whole nation, turned Israel into defeat, and brought all of Israel guilty before God, and God withheld His blessing upon them!

The whole scenario is explained in James 1:14, 15. (Put 'Achan' in the midst of what James says and insert the word covetousness for lust.) "Every man is tempted, when he is drawn away of his own lusts [covetousness] and enticed. Then when lust [covetousness] hath conceived, it brings forth sin, and sin, when it is finished, brings forth death." Achan looked, desired [coveted], took the forbidden items, and was sentenced to die. God demanded a complete and thorough "cleansing." When the sin [covetousness, which was disobedience to God's command] was dealt with and put away, God turned from the fierceness of His anger and judgment to again restore His power and blessing upon Israel. Now, what does this say to us today? What can we learn from this dreadful act of covetousness?

There is no alternative to obedience. God and sin cannot co-exist. If we are to be led by Him and blessed with His Presence and Power, we must deal with, confess to, and repent of sin. How clearly God reveals His grace to those who covet. "Return, thou backsliding sinner, says the Lord, and I will not cause mine anger to fall upon you; for I am merciful, says the Lord, and I will not keep mine anger forever; only acknowledge your iniquity." It is not for us to alter in any way what God has clearly set forth in His Word. We must follow in explicit obedience, focusing our lives on HIS WORD and HIS WILL, and seek to be led in HIS WAY! Fix your eyes upon Jesus!

I Have Overcome the World

"In this world you will have trouble. But take heart! I have overcome the world." John 16:33

*W*hat consolation do you have as you face everyday demands and the insidious ways of Satan? God has given the Believer a Covenant that is steadfast and all-sufficient, encompasses our every need, and is irrevocable. His promises are sure and true, exceeding great and precious, "that by these we may be partakers of the divine nature." To rest in His provisions is to experience "conquering faith" and an intimate relationship with the Lord that is known only by those who "dare to believe" in the midst of the conflicts of life. How can we possibly read in Hebrews 11 of the persevering, triumphant faith of these battle-scarred warriors, who through adversity we know nothing of, "endured, as looking for a city whose builder and maker was God." Think through the words of the writer of Hebrews 11.

"And what shall I say more? For time would fail me to tell of Gideon, of Barak, of Samson, of Jephthae, of David, of Samuel, and of the prophets. Through faith, they subdued kingdoms, wrought righteousness, obtained promises, stopped the mouths of lions, quenched the violence of fire, escaped the edge of the sword, were made strong out of weakness, waxed valiant in battle, and turned to flight the armies of the aliens. Women received their dead raised to life again; others were tortured, not accepting deliverance, so that they might obtain a better resurrection. And others had trial of cruel mockery and scourging, yea, moreover of bonds and imprisonment. They were stoned, they were sawn asunder, were tempted, were slain with the sword: they wandered about in sheepskins, being destitute, afflicted, and tormented. (Of whom this world is not worthy.) They wandered in deserts and in mountains and in dens and caves."

What is Paul's challenge to us today? He says, "Wherefore, seeing we are compassed about with so great a cloud of witnesses, let us lay aside every weight, and the sin that doth so easily beset us, and let us run with patience [with perseverance, with determination, with purpose, with dedicated commitment] the race that is set before us, looking unto Jesus, the author and finisher of our faith." Then he tells us what to do. "Lift up the hands that hang down, and the feeble knees, and make straight paths for your feet, lest that which is lame be turned out of the way, but let them rather be healed. Follow peace with all men and holiness, without which no man shall see God."

Finally, he instructs us, "Let us go forth unto Him, without the camp, bearing His reproach. Let us offer the sacrifice of praise to God continually, that is, the fruit of our lips giving thanks to His name." To "go forth unto Him without the camp" means to identify with Him in His shameful rejection by those who refuse to submit to the authority of God and refuse the Lordship of Christ. This is the place where every committed Believer should be, by the side of our blessed Saviour. Where do we stand amidst a "holy scene" like this? Demonstrated commitment is not merely an "outward profession," but the "reality of an inward possession" where Christ sits upon the throne of our heart as SOVEREIGN! God has called us to personal holiness, which demonstrates the Presence of Christ in our lives. Persevere with purpose, LOOKING UNTO JESUS!

Apart to Pray...
Alone With God

"And when he had sent the multitudes away, he went up into a mountain apart to pray: and when the evening was come, he was there alone." Matthew 14:23

It is interesting to notice that after Jesus had fed the 5,000, He sent his disciples to the other side of the lake ahead of Him, and then He sent the multitudes away. Why? He was separating Himself from everything that would be a hindrance to the solitude He desired when He communed with the Father. Then, "He went up into a mountain apart to pray: and when the evening was come, He was there alone." Pressed and pursued at every turn, it was imperative for Jesus to have His time of rest and solitude with the Father, a time of being alone with God, being refreshed and renewed.

Someone has said, "There is no music in a rest, but there is the 'making' of music in it." In a musical score, you often will find a little symbol that is called a "rest." It indicates to the musician that he is to stop playing for the time indicated by that symbol. It is not a note to be played, but a silence to be observed. In its silence, it has various effects on the music being played. It could bring a striking crescendo into silence, and accentuate the dramatic effect. It could emphasize the melodious quietness of a peaceful melody, when everything stops and you drink in the solemn beauty of its restful tones. Such is the picture that David sought to portray when he wrote, "Be still and know that I am God."

Can you imagine how much God would reveal of Himself if we were "alone" with Him? This is our privilege when He instructs us to "be still and know that I am God." It is there that we enter into the "holy of holies," the "secret place of His tabernacle." That is where David retreated, time and again. It was there that his strength was renewed, his courage made strong, his faith replenished, his vision made clear, his heart made pure, and his spirit fixed upon God in unwavering confidence! He "came apart" even as Jesus did, and communed with God! He has provided a refuge for us, the "secret privacy" of His presence. Oh that we would develop the lost art of "meditation" and the culture of being "alone with God" in the holy silence and beauty of His Presence!

We find so many illustrations that portray this blessed place in the presence of God. Have you ever been overwhelmed by the awesome quietness and the majestic splendour of the Swiss Alps, or the serene beauty of the Blue Ridge Mountains, or the quiet stillness of a beautiful lake? Think of the grandeur and power of the ocean as its waves crash endlessly upon the white sands of the beach. All of these inviting scenes magnify the greatness of God, but they also portray the "glory of being alone with Him in the secret of His presence." I never cease to stand in awe when I realize that God has provided that holy of holies for every Believer, whereby we may enter into the very PRESENCE OF GOD! I cannot begin to comprehend how great a blessing this is for every Believer! How much time are you spending in the secret privacy of His Presence, all alone with God? He is waiting for you to come and commune with Him so that He may reveal Himself anew and afresh!

Grace Increased All the More

"Where sin increased, grace increased all the more: so that, just as sin reigned unto death, so also grace might reign through righteousness to bring eternal life through Jesus Christ our Lord." Romans 5:20- 21

Only one thing exceeds the depth of our sin, iniquity, and rebellion against God, and that is the exceeding Greatness of God's Condescending Love. However great is the depth of our sin, God's love reaches even lower and Forgives, Redeems, Restores, and Reconciles us unto Himself. Who can fathom God's abounding Love, His amazing grace, and His Mercy that is exceedingly great? Read prayerfully the words of this beloved hymn we sing. May the truth of its message inscribe itself upon our hearts and instill a confident trust in an ever-faithful loving God.

> Marvelous grace of our loving Lord, grace that exceeds our sin and our guilt,
> Yonder on Calvary's mount outpoured, there where the blood of the Lamb was spilt.
> Sin and despair like the sea waves cold, threaten the soul with infinite loss.
> Grace that is greater, yes, grace untold, points to the Refuge, the mighty Cross.
> Dark is the stain that we cannot hide; what can avail to wash it away?

Look! There is flowing a crimson tide; whiter than snow you may be
   today.
Marvelous, Infinite, Matchless Grace, freely bestowed to all who
   believe,
You that are longing to see His face, will you this moment His grace
   receive?
Grace, Grace, God's Grace... Grace that that will pardon and cleanse
   within.
Grace, Grace, God's Grace... Grace that is Greater than All Our Sin!

How great is His Love and Grace? (James 4:6) "Where sin
abounded, grace did much more abound." (Romans 5:2) Read
prayerfully the words of Annie Johnson Flint:

He giveth more grace when the burdens grow greater.
   He sendeth more strength when the labours increase.
To added affliction He addeth His Mercy.
   To multiplied trials His multiplied peace.
When we have exhausted our storehouse of endurance,
   When our strength is failed ere the day is half done,
When we reach the end of our hoarded resources,
   Our Father's full giving has only begun.
His Love has no limit, His Grace has no measure.
   His Power has no boundary known unto men.
For out of His Infinite Riches in Jesus,
   He Giveth... and Giveth... and Giveth Again!

Sometimes we wonder in our distress, "Where is God when I
need Him?" Well, He's right where I left Him! When we are faced
with devastating circumstances, we should not look at the circumstances for the answer we need and wonder, "Where is God?" We
need to look within and find where we have separated ourselves
from the presence and power of God through our sinful neglect, or
from following our own self-centered ways. With a broken heart
and a contrite spirit that finds ourselves at the foot of the Cross in
repentance and confession, we will experience His Forgiveness. He
is ever willing to restore, bind up, and receive us back again in full
fellowship with Him by God's Great Grace! Marvelous, Matchless,
Infinite grace!

For I Know Him

"For I know him, that he will command his children and his household after him, and they shall keep the way of the Lord, to do justice and judgment." Genesis 18:19

*I*t is always challenging to read how God worked through ordinary men in the days of the Prophets and Apostles. Especially when you keep in mind the circumstances that surrounded their lives. It makes their encounters with God all the more amazing. The verse before us concerns Abraham, that great man of faith who walked with God and was called a friend of God. God said, "I know him." Let's look at one incident in his life.

Abraham came from a family and country that were idolatrous. There was nothing spectacular in Abraham's life that would attract man, much less God. But in His providence, "God chose Abraham." He had a plan and purpose for Abraham like He had for no other. Through Abraham, all the nations of the earth were to be blessed. His seed would be as "the sand of the sea." Through him the "Seed of the Promised Messiah" was to come. Before God begins to initiate His plan, God reveals Himself to Abraham as "El Shaddai", Almighty God. He is the One who nourishes, the Strength Giver, the Satisfier who pours Himself into believing lives. The One Ever Faithful who makes our lives fruitful. This was very important to Abraham. God wants to establish in Abraham's heart the right concept of God.

Immediately afterward, God says unto Abraham concerning Sarah, "And I will bless her, and give thee a son also of her." Can you imagine the consternation of Abraham? "Lord, I'm 75 years old and Sarah..." "Yes, I know how old both of you are, but I'm going to give you a son." What do you think Sarah's reaction was when he told her? Abraham, have you lost your mind? I'm sure when the word got around, everybody was asking Abraham, "Where is this promised son, Abe? You know you and Sarah are rather old. How long will it be before your son is born?"

With a gleam in his eye, He would answer, "Do you see those hills? One day they are going to belong to my descendants." "But Abe, you don't have any children. How can you say such a thing?" "True, but God has promised me a son, and we believe God that it shall be even as it was told us."

Abraham had a "futuristic faith." He took God at His word and believed Him with unreserved faith. God had said that through him all the nations of the earth would be blessed, and it could only happen through the birth of a son given to him by God. Abraham had a Biblical faith that dared to launch out into uncharted waters and believe the impossible. God had said of Abraham, "For I know him." Wow! What a testimony! Does God look at your life and mine and know us in such a way? Does He see us as ones He can trust to stand faithfully amid the swirling waves of doubt, criticism, and abuse by an unbelieving world? Can He see us "daring to believe" and taking Him at His word, going forth unto "adventures of faith" for His glory?

Abraham believed God when he could not see any evidence to encourage him. May He find each of us with hungry hearts and responsive spirits, ready to answer even as Isaiah did, "Here am I Lord; send me."

Do Not Drift Away

"We must pay more careful attention, therefore, to what we have heard, so that we do not drift away." Hebrews 2:1

*I*t was a time of great prosperity and a golden age, more than Israel had ever known, except during Solomon's reign. At least that is how it appeared on the outside. Within, there was moral decay slowly eating away every fiber of hope and relationship they had ever known with Jehovah. Flagrant injustice by those in authority, inhumane treatment of the poor and needy, discrimination and greed by the rich, and a total disregard to all that were not in the inner circle. Their worship was an abomination. Prostitution and homosexuality abounded within the Temple. Their own children were sacrificed to the gods. All of these actions pointed to the utter disregard of Jehovah.

How could people fall to such a diabolical state of sin after they had been miraculously delivered from the bondage of Egypt; had been led, protected, and provided for by God for 40 years in the wilderness; had been led into the promised land; and had seen time and again the mighty power of God manifested for them?

One of the stories that came out of World War II was about a Navy cruiser that was anchored in the Azores, off the coast of Spain. It has been told that the sailors on watch asked a group of Army infantrymen, who happened to be on board, to "stand watch" while they went below for a meal. The soldiers were more than willing to help. Unfortunately, they were untrained for their new responsibility. They were unaware that the ship's anchor was not secure and that the ship was gradually drifting toward shallow water. A trained seaman knows to periodically check a stationary landmark to keep tabs on the stability of the ship's anchorage. Within an hour, the ship had drifted against a line of rocks. Minutes later, a wave lifted the ship onto the rocks, ripping a hole in the bow. An alarm was sounded and the ship was evacuated. As the big cruiser heaved to one side, some of the equipment on deck collided and caught fire. Soon the entire vessel was engulfed in flames and sank.

Each day, we all battle an "unseen current" that leads to utter destruction and makes us susceptible to the infiltrating ways of Satan. We must be constantly aware that the effects of the tide can move us away from God. We need to focus on Christ, and watch the compass to chart our course. We have a tendency to drift toward where we focus our attention. If the soldiers on deck had focused their attention on a fixed position on shore to check the ship's movement, they could have avoided disaster. The focus of our attention determines our life's direction. When we are too busy to pray, neglect reading the Bible, and fail to spend time with God, we're not only too busy, but we are drifting slowly but surely to spiritual disaster. We become insensitive to the Holy Spirit and unresponsive to His drawing us to Christ. Our hearts become dull and cold and we, like Peter, will follow afar off. "We must pay more careful attention, therefore, to what we have heard, so we will not drift away." Jesus Christ is the Lighthouse that warns us of danger, but also gives us the direction of our course. I trust the focus of our lives may be "LOOKING UNTO JESUS, the Author and Finisher of Our Life."

You Knew My Path

"I poured out my complaint before him; I showed before him my trouble. When my spirit was overwhelmed within me, then you knew my path." Psalm 142:2-3

The many encounters David experienced with Saul's men as they were constantly in hot pursuit of him brought him humbly before God, realizing his weakness and utmost need to find his refuge in the Lord. He learns to lean upon God for his strength, intervention, and sufficiency. Completely overwhelmed, David cries unto the Lord, and bares his heart and soul. Convinced that the Lord knew all about his devastating circumstances and would be his comfort and companion through it all, he goes forth in renewed courage. He trusts God to work in and through him for His Glory, regardless of the circumstances. We can learn from David's varied experiences. Although he fell to great depths, he found through heart-rending repentance the merciful grace of God to forgive and raise him up to be a "man after God's own heart."

How often we cry out for deliverance, because of our difficulty or devastating circumstances, discouraged in spirit, weak in faith, resting in our own weakness, and mulling in defeat. May we know the strength and power of the Holy Spirit that dwells within us and makes us triumphant wherever we are placed by God. He enables us to reflect His Love and Grace, amidst the ugliness and sin that surrounds us, to keep us pure and radiant for His Glory. Forbid that we should turn from His working, or shun that which will conform us to the image of His Son and into a deeper and a more intimate relationship to the Lord. God has given you a ministry in which He will enable and empower you to be an effective channel of blessing where you are. Let Him fill you with His presence in a new and living way by His Spirit. He knows our hearts and will faithfully guide us in the "path of righteousness for His name's sake."

Often the path leads us into areas of deep concern, danger, and perplexing circumstances. This was the challenge of five devoted young missionaries who "dared to believe" in God's Hand and Purpose in it all. God had laid upon their hearts to carry the Gospel to the Stone Age tribe of Auca Indians in the dense jungles of Ecuador. With thorough preparation and planning, they were ready to make contact with savage Indians they had never met, for whom they had prayed for six years, and for whom they were willing to give their lives to reach with the saving grace of God's Word. As they waited on the white sand on the banks of the Curaray River, they were in the silent world of hostile Indians who were feared by everyone because of their instinct to kill anyone who invaded their forbidden land. But they were "under the shadow of His wings" on a mission that would resound throughout eternity. Then on Sunday, Jan. 8, 1956, the men they sought to reach killed them. Jim Elliot, Nate Saint, and Ed McCulley had been classmates of mine at Wheaton College. You say, "How tragic!" No, this was the path of life God had chosen for them. Through their martyrdom, the Gospel has been planted into the hearts of countless souls around the world, and untold doors of opportunity have been opened. Only Eternity will reveal the impact of their lives and the reality of Jim Elliot's words: "He is no fool who gives what he cannot keep, to gain what he cannot lose."

We Have This Ministry

"Therefore, seeing we have this ministry, as we have received mercy, we faint not." 2 Corinthians 4:1

*O*ur commitment to God is in direct proportion to our concept of the Majesty of God. Our concept of the Majesty of God is in direct proportion to how receptive and responsive we are to the Holy Spirit. You say, "How can that be?" Let's look into our lives and see how God has worked.

It was the Holy Spirit that awakened us to our sinful state before a holy God. Our sin had separated us from God, and the Holy Spirit revealed to us God's only provision for reconciliation, Jesus Christ, our Saviour. As we were receptive to His probing and responsive to His revelation of this truth, we confessed and repented of our sin and He made us a new creation in Christ. Being God's child, He desires to bring our lives into conformity to His Will, so that we may glorify Him in our life and know the joy, peace, and power of God in our Spiritual Journey. By the Holy Spirit, He begins to reveal WHO GOD IS, His Holiness, His Righteousness, His Justice, His Love, His Grace, and His Mercy. As we are receptive to the Holy Spirit, we respond in the surrender of Our Will to His Authority and Sovereignty that leads to our commitment and dedication of heart and life to Christ. It is in this process that the Holy Sprit gives unto us a continuing, increasing measure, a CONCEPT OF THE MAJESTY OF GOD.

Paul is saying, "The Holy Spirit, having revealed unto me in a most convincing manner, God's tender mercies and grace, I am constrained by the love of God to this ministry He has committed unto us; we faint not." But you say, "What ministry has God committed unto me?" Only you can answer that. He has a ministry for you.

One of the most blessed and needful ministries that comes to my mind, and one in which you can be wonderfully used, is TO BE AN ENCOURAGER. One who is willing to come alongside of someone else and assure him that you care and want to share the great need in his life and be compassionate. That means literally "to suffer with," sharing in the suffering passion of another. This means so much more than a mere sympathetic word or a show of pity. You identify with the person whose heart is broken, whose body is wracked with pain, whose hope is seemingly lost, where tragedy has struck and the person knows not where to turn or what to do. Compassion extends a loving heart and holds back the quick, eager explanations we are so prone to offer. Rather, it means opening yourself up to another's pain and hurt, and sharing their tears of sorrow or quiet sadness. People on every side are in devastating need; they long for someone to be an encouragement to them, to manifest the love of God to them. Such a ministry can be yours! Paul said, "Seeing we have this ministry, because we have been the recipients of the abounding mercy and grace of God, WE FAINT NOT." We will not fail or shrink from the ministry God has given unto us. YOU CAN BE AN ENCOURAGER, ONE WHO WILL COME ALONGSIDE OF OTHERS IN THEIR GREAT NEED! "For I the Lord thy God will hold thy right hand, saying unto thee, Fear not; I will help thee."

There Remains Yet the Youngest

"So he asked Jesse, 'Are these all the sons you have?' 'There is still the youngest,' Jesse answered, 'but he is tending the sheep.' Samuel said, 'Send for him; we will not sit down until he arrives.' Then the Lord said, 'Rise, anoint him; he is the one.'" 1 Samuel 16:11,12

God had dethroned Saul as King of Israel, because of his disobedience and rejection of God. God tells Samuel to go to the house of Jesse, and from his sons, He will find the "man after God's own heart" who is to be anointed the new King of Israel. Seven of Jesse's sons appear before Samuel, but none is God's choice. Then Samuel asks, "Are these all the sons you have?" To which Jesse answers, "There remains yet the youngest." "And where do we find him?" "Out in the field tending the sheep." It was David, a young man with a shepherd's heart. He has been trained in all the tender and sensitive ways of caring for the sheep. God says to Samuel, "Rise, anoint him: for this is the one." How blessed to have the mind of the Lord and be led by Him.

What was wrong with the other sons? One in particular illustrates God's heart. Eliab came before Samuel, a strong, strapping, handsome man who certainly would have been the choice of most. But Samuel said he was not the one. Then God tells Samuel His clarifying thought: "Look not on his countenance or on the height of his stature, because I have refused him; for the Lord sees not as man sees; for man looks on the outward appearance, but God looks on the heart." God ignores what Man glories in. David was looked upon as insignificant, unworthy, too young, and unqualified, but He was God's chosen one. "My thoughts are not your thoughts, neither are my ways your ways, saith the Lord."

Look who God had chosen before: Abraham, from an idolatrous family and nation; Isaac, not Ishmael, Abraham's first-born son; Jacob, not Esau, the first-born of Isaac; Moses, a shepherd on the backside of the desert; Israel, not Egypt, the Babylonians, or the Greeks (each representing commendable strength, wisdom, and culture). WHY? So that all men might know, "Power belonged unto the Lord. His ways are past finding out, and He doeth all things after the counsel of His own will."

Tony Campolo, in "*Stories for a Man's Heart*," compiled by Al and Alice Gray, tells of a young cerebral palsy victim at a junior high school camp, who was the brunt of others' jokes and the object of their laughter. Billy moved with an uncoordinated body. He spoke in slow, stammering words from a contorted mouth. The others would mimic Billy's stammering speech. "It's ... over ... there, ... Billy." The fury reached its highest point when Billy was told that he was to give the cabin devotions. I knew when they chose him that they just wanted to make fun of him. Billy dragged himself to the front amid giggles that were everywhere. It took him almost five minutes to say seven words: "JESUS ... LOVES ... ME ... AND ... I ... LOVE ... JESUS!" There was dead silence, and then tears streamed down the faces of all of the kids. A revival broke out all over the camp. God had used a "cerebral palsy kid" to do what the testimonies of sports figures could not do. He chose an afflicted, outcast, distorted, and stammering boy to break the hearts of the haughty. "God said unto Samuel, Rise, anoint him: for this is the one." DARE TO BELIEVE!

To order additional copies of

Dare To Trust

Or its companion book

DARE TO BELIEVE
(available in Spring 2006)

Or please visit our web site at

www.xulonpress.com